HALIFAX
A COLOUR GUIDEBOOK

Stephen Poole
Photography by Keith Vaughan

FORMAC PUBLISHING COMPANY LIMITED
HALIFAX

For Matthew Francis

Canadian Cataloging in Publication Data
Poole, Stephen, 1963-
Halifax
ISBN 0-88780-320-2
1. Halifax (N.S.) — Guidebooks. I. Vaughan, Keith, 1943-
II. Title
FC2346.18.P66 1995   917.16'225044   C95-950097-9
F1039.5.H17P66 1995

Formac Publishing Company Limited
5502 Atlantic Street
Halifax B3H 1G4

Distributed in the United States by
Formac Distributing Limited
121 Mount Vernon Street
Boston MA 02108

Printed and bound in Canada

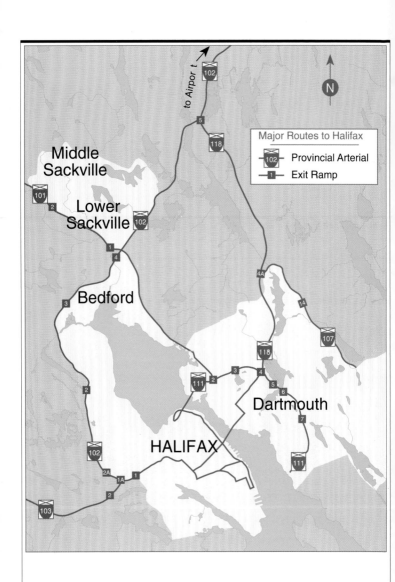

ROUTE MAP LEGEND

1 Citadel Hill
2 Downtown
3 Spring Garden Road
4 South End and Point Pleasant Park
5 Dartmouth

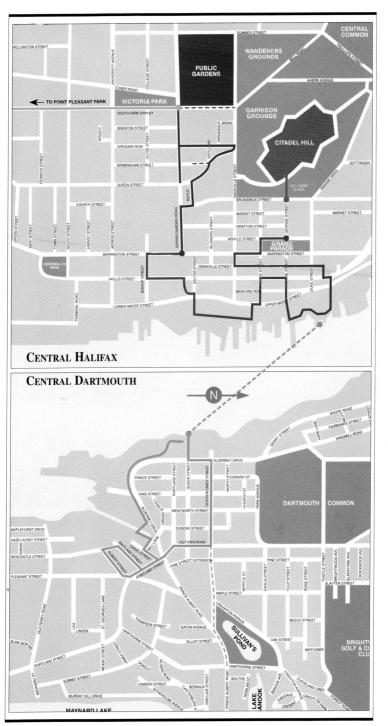

Central Halifax

Central Dartmouth

ABOVE: TOWN CRIER

RIGHT: AERIAL VIEW OF CITADEL HILL

HALIFAX: AN INTRODUCTION

For much of its life, Halifax has been a garrison town. It was established in 1749 to counter the military threat posed by the French Fortress of Louisbourg on Île-Royale (Cape Breton Island). When Louisbourg fell in 1758, the British turned their attention to Quebec; preparations for the seige were made in Halifax. And so it went. Halifax served as a British stronghold during the American Revolution and throughout the Napoleonic Wars. Whenever British interests in North America seemed threatened, Halifax's fortifications were strengthened. Standing guard over the harbour and the naval dockyard, the fortresses atop Citadel Hill grew increasingly elaborate.

SEA KING HELICOPTERS OVER THE HARBOUR

This century, Halifax has remained stalwart in the face of new adversaries, the magnificent harbour having served as a marshalling area for North Atlantic convoys during two World Wars.

There is still a strong military presence in the city. Warships regularly ply the harbour; overhead, are aircraft on their way to or from the Canadian Forces Base at Shearwater. And sailors from the NATO fleet are regular visitors.

Yet, Halifax is no longer a primarily military town. Since the Second World War, rapid growth in the research, transportation, and public service sectors has turned the old garrison town into a vital commercial and government centre. The port's two container terminals handle international cargoes. The provincial legislature is here, and the city is home to a substantial federal bureaucracy. Many of the 115,000 people in Halifax and the more than 300,000 in the metropolitan area work for the government or in government-related service industries.

At first glance, Halifax can easily be mistaken for a staid, provincial town where commerce, government, and the military set the tone. But don't let the city fool you. There is a thriving alternative scene here. Recently, local bands like Sloan had music critics touting Halifax as a possible successor to Seattle as North America's next hip city. For years, the students and faculty at the Nova Scotia College of Art and Design (NSCAD) have been leading the way for movements like conceptual art. You will find their work on display at the Anna Leonowens Gallery (Tour 2), on Granville Street. The city's six universities, including NSCAD, resist cultural complacency.

CHEAPSIDE, SITE OF THE ART GALLERY OF NOVA SCOTIA

So, Halifax is Janus-faced. The military is here but so is Vajradhatu, the headquarters for an international network of Buddhist meditation centres. As you walk downtown, look for the independent bookstores, coffee shops, gift stores, and galleries that are tucked in among the office towers.

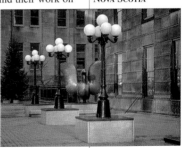

HALIFAX HARBOUR

The city's outstanding resource is its harbour. Extending inland about 16 km (10 mi.) from its seaward approaches, it is the second largest natural harbour in the world. The harbour, like much of Nova Scotia's Atlantic coast, was

formed by glacial erosion and the ensuing rise in sea level caused by glacial meltwater at the end of the last ice age (to learn more about the province's natural history, visit the Nova Scotia Museum of Natural History on Summer Street). Now, the harbour remains ice-free except for the occasional short-lived episode during exceptionally hard winters.

ARMDALE YACHT CLUB

The harbour, and the sea beyond, affects every aspect of city life. It does this in obvious ways: its shipping lanes are essential to commerce; it moderates the city's climate, freshening the warmest summer days with sea breezes and taking the edge off winter cold snaps; and it is a source of recreation and pleasure for Haligonians and visitors alike (the harbour's Bedford Basin and its Northwest Arm are summer yachting havens).

But the harbour also lends more subtle flavours to life along its shores. In downtown businesses it often takes several promotions to get an office with a harbour view. Together with Citadel Hill, the harbour serves as a reference for everything else in the city. And it is there in every outdoor breath you take in Halifax.

To get the most out of your visit, arrange to get out on the water. The Halifax-Dartmouth Ferry (Tour 5) provides one of the best and cheapest ways to see the harbour and both shorelines, while a variety of private charters and harbour tours leave from Cable Wharf (Tour 2), in downtown Halifax.

ORIGINS

Centuries before the Europeans arrived, the Mi'kmaq had been spending summers along the shores of Chebuktook, "the biggest harbour". For a few short months, warm weather and an abundance of shorebirds and fish made this a most

hospitable place. Then, the Mi'kmaq would paddle and portage their way across the mainland to return to their winter camps along the more sheltered Bay of Fundy.

European fishermen made similar use of the harbour. It was a convenient port of call during the fishing season. In 1698, the French established a fishing station in Chebuktook on what is now McNab's Island, but permanent settlement awaited a bold British move in their 18th-century chess match with the French.

In 1744 France declared war on Britain. In the New World, Massachusetts governor William Shirley saw this as an opportunity to seize control of the rich Louisbourg fishery from the French. In 1745, a group of 4000 New England militiamen supported by a British naval squadron attacked the fortress. To everyone's surprise, the "Dunkirk of the West" fell after a 46-day siege.

During the intense negotiations that followed the end of the war in 1748, the British sacrificed Louisbourg in order to hold on to some of their European gains. The following year, Louisbourg was returned to the French. But the British had awakened to the strategic importance of Nova Scotia (in large part, as a result of the angry shouts of New Englanders). It could protect New England from any French designs on the territory.

So, the colonization and fortification of Nova Scotia became part of British policy. In June of 1749, Colonel Edward Cornwallis and 3000 settlers arrived at Chebuktook.

Although Cornwallis doubted the mettle of the new colonists (most were disbanded soldiers and sailors), he had no doubts about the site chosen for the new colony.

THORNDEAN ON INGLIS STREET (1834)

ST. PAUL'S ANGLICAN CHURCH

He and his officers agreed that the harbour was the finest they had ever seen. Halifax, named after the head of the Board of Trade and Plantations in London, was built on the harbour's western shore.

From the top of Citadel Hill you can look down the slope toward the harbour, at the original townsite. From the Grand Parade, the public square between Barrington and Argyle streets, surveyor Charles Morris divided the ground into lots to accommodate the town's first settlers. At the south end of the square, St. Paul's Anglican Church (Tour 2), completed in 1750, was Halifax's first building. South of the church, at the foot of Spring Garden Road, is the Old Burying Ground (Tour 3), the town's original cemetery.

SEBASTOPOL MONUMENT AT THE OLD BURYING GROUND

Dartmouth was founded in 1750. Two years later, John Connor began operating his harbour ferry service (Connor died in 1754; his gravestone can be seen in the Old Burying Ground). The Halifax-Dartmouth Ferry has been running ever since.

ROYAL LIAISONS

Halifax received royal attention toward the end of the 18th century. In 1786, Prince William (later, King William IV) of the Royal Navy came to town. He was a scallywag whose chief occupations were boozing and philandering. In Halifax,

he met the Wentworths — John and his ambitious wife Frances. William and Frances struck up a relationship that scandalized Halifax Society, but did nothing to harm John's political aspirations. He became Lieutenant-Governor of Nova Scotia in 1792, whereupon he and his wife began scheming to upgrade their accommodations. Today, you can see

PRINCE OF WALES TOWER, POINT PLEASANT PARK

the fruits of their labour at Government House (Tour 2), a beautiful Georgian building in the Palladian style, on the corner of Bishop and Barrington streets.

Although the Wentworths' extravagant new home made the government wary of expenditures on public buildings, the new home of the legislature, Province House (Tour 2), was certainly not compromised. Opened in 1819, it is one of the finest examples of Georgian architecture in Canada.

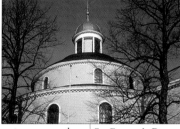

Halifax's second royal visitor, Prince Edward, was a saint compared to his brother. He assumed command of the garrison at Halifax in 1794 and immediately set to work strengthening the town's fortifications. He expanded the fortress atop Citadel Hill. He built Martello towers at Point Pleasant Park (Tour 4), York Redoubt (overlooking the western approaches of the harbour), and McNab's Island (now the site of a lighthouse). And, he established Royal Artillery Park (Tour 3) to the south of Citadel Hill.

The Prince did much more than fortify the town. He refined it. He built St. George's Round Church to

ST. GEORGE'S ROUND CHURCH BEFORE THE FIRE

PRINCE'S LODGE ROTUNDA, BEDFORD BASIN

BELOW: OLD TOWN CLOCK

accommodate the overflow from the "Little Dutch Church" at the corner of Brunswick and Cornwallis streets (Edward shared German roots with the congregation). Tragically, St. George's was destroyed by fire in the summer of 1994, but plans to rebuild are underway. He also built a round, ornamental garden temple at his estate along the shores of the Bedford Basin. Visible from the Bedford Highway, the building is not open to the public, but you are welcomed to stroll through the hemlock ravine opposite the rotunda. There, you will find heart-shaped Julie's Pond, named for Edward's French mistress. Legend has it that the paths that once meandered through the estate spelled out her name.

Prince Edward's final gift to Halifax became its most enduring landmark, the Old Town Clock (Tour 1) at the base of Citadel Hill.

PRESS GANGS AND PRIVATEERS

A good war could make the reputation of a prince, but for some, warfare brought nothing but trouble. The admiral needed men to serve in His Majesty's Navy. In Halifax, like everywhere else, there was no rush of volunteers, so the admiral turned to the ruling council for the press warrant that would allow his press gangs to "recruit" sailors. They were usually given 24 hours to roam the downtown streets, often cudgelling young men into service. Understandably, morale in the Navy was low.

There were deserters and mutineers, but not many. The Navy made sure of this. In the summer of 1809, six mutineers from the *Columbine* were hung in chains on Mauger's Beach near the present site of the McNab's Island lighthouse. They were neither the first nor the last to die on "Hangman's Beach".

Other Haligonians profited from the wars. Privateers received letters of marque from the government, licensing

them to plunder enemy ships. It was a lucrative business, and nobody was better at it than Liverpool, Nova Scotia native, Enos Collins. His *Liverpool Packet* terrorized merchant shipping off the New England coast during the War of 1812. Collins built a financial empire on privateers' booty. When he died in 1871 aged 99, he was thought to be the richest man in Canada.

Today, the waterfront warehouse where Collins stored his loot is part of Historic Properties (Tour 2). The collection of ten buildings from the Georgian and early Victorian periods houses restaurants, boutiques, offices, and taverns.

SIMON'S BUILDING AT HISTORIC PROPERTIES

BELOW:
SHUBENACADIE CANAL INTERPRETIVE CENTRE

PUBLIC WORKS

There was no war to drive the Halifax economy during the middle of the 19th century. Instead, there were two

massive construction projects, the fourth fortress on Citadel Hill (Tour 1), and the Shubenacadie Canal (Tour 5), which linked Halifax Harbour to the Bay of Fundy.

These two undertakings were similar. Both took a great deal of time to build — the fortress from 1828-56, and the canal from 1826-61. Both employed hundreds of labourers and skilled artisans. And both were obsolete upon completion; the fort rendered largely useless by the advent of long-range, rifled naval guns, and the canal quickly replaced by the new Intercolonial Railway.

Ironically, both enterprises have succeeded admirably as tourist attractions. The Citadel is the most visited national historic site in Canada and should be near the top of your list of things to see in Halifax. The canal works remain a source of fascination at the Shubenacadie Canal Interpretive Centre (Tour 5) on Alderney Drive in Dartmouth and the Fairbanks Interpretive Centre in Shubie Park on the Waverley Road (Route 318).

SOUTH PARK STREET RESIDENCE

VICTORIAN HALIFAX

Halifax prospered during the second half of the 19th century. Although the steamships of Samuel Cunard's line soon stopped calling at Halifax (they quickly outgrew the city), they remained shining examples of what a local boy could do when he put his mind to it. Entrepreneurs like George Wright conducted business from the modern new buildings on Barrington Street (Tour 2). Lavish Victorian mansions were built along Young Avenue (Tour 4).

BANDSTAND AT THE PUBLIC GARDENS

ANCHOR SHAFT OF THE *MONT BLANC*

While the Halifax elite did well at business, they excelled at leisure. Respectable ladies and gentlemen took Sunday afternoon strolls through Point Pleasant Park (Tour 4) or picnicked on McNab's Island. Dalhousie College, now Dalhousie University, offered lectures for their edification. Regattas were held at the Royal Nova Scotia Yacht Squadron. Concerts were given by students and faculty at the Academy of Music. And Anna Leonowens, the governess immortalized in the Rodgers and Hammerstein musical *The King and I*, helped to establish the high-minded Victoria School of Art and Design (Tour 2).

Nowhere was this Victorian refinement more evident than at the Public Gardens (Tour 3), adjacent to Spring Garden Road. Today, these formal Victorian gardens are the oldest — many say the finest — in North America.

TWO WORLD WARS

After a century of peace, Halifax was once again at war in 1914. Old patterns were repeated. The population swelled with the arrival of thousands of military personnel and civilian workers. Camp followers came in droves, earning decent livings from the sale of booze and sex. Harbour defences were shored up. And British warships filled the harbour (at the outbreak of the First World War, Canada's navy consisted of one near-derelict ship, the *Niobe*).

SPRING GARDEN ROAD

Halifax's great wartime disaster was the result of a navigational blunder, not a German attack. On December 6, 1917, the French steamship *Mont Blanc*, loaded with explosives, collided with the Belgian steamer *Imo*. The resulting blast levelled the north ends of both Halifax and Dartmouth, killing nearly 2000 people; many others were blinded or maimed. The Maritime Museum of the Atlantic (Tour 2), on Lower Water Street, gives a poignant account of the Explosion while telling much of Halifax's seafaring story.

During the Second World War, more than 17,000 ships left in convoy from Halifax. A submarine net was stretched across the harbour mouth to prevent U-boat attacks. The Germans did manage to sink one merchant ship at the

approaches to the harbour, but, once again, the real damage to the city was the result of friendly fire. This time, V-E Day celebrations turned ugly and downtown Halifax was the scene of a full-scale riot. Thousands of sailors stormed liquor stores and breweries. Thousands more civilians joined in the drunkenness, fornication, and looting. It was, in the words of Nova Scotia novelist and historian Thomas Raddall, "a scene for Hogarth" (*Halifax: Warden of the North*).

DIVERSIONS

If you spend any length of time in the city, then you will probably want to do some shopping. The best shops are found along Spring Garden Road (Tour 3) and in Historic Properties (Tour 2). Look for the quality work of Nova Scotia craftspeople at Jennifer's of Nova Scotia (Tour 3), the Micmac Heritage Gallery (Tour 2), and the Gallery Shop (Tour 2) at the Art Gallery of Nova Scotia

NOVA SCOTIA COLLEGE OF ART AND DESIGN, GRANVILLE STREET

LEFT: BUSKER AND FRIEND

(while here, check out the outstanding collection of Nova Scotia folk art). You will also find a large selection of craft items on display, though not for sale, at the Nova Scotia Centre for Craft and Design (Tour 2) on Barrington Street.

It is a rare summer day in the Halifax area when there is no special event or festival taking place (for complete listings, consult the *Nova Scotia Travel Guide*, available at any Visitor Information Centre). One of the major attractions is the Nova Scotia International Tattoo, a musical extravaganza with a military flavour which runs for a week in July at the Metro Centre. The Atlantic Jazz Festival (late July) and Dartmouth's Maritime Old Time Fiddling Contest and Jamboree (mid-July) are both top-notch musical events with little else in common. Each August, street

AFRICVILLE REUNION

performers gather along the waterfront and on city sidewalks to join in the International Buskerfest. The Greek Festival (early June) and the Africville Reunion (late July) are two popular events with a multicultural theme. Chances are you will find a festival that enhances your stay in Halifax.

CITADEL HILL

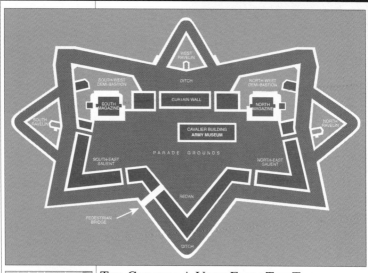

HARBOUR SLOPE OF THE CITADEL, THEN AND NOW

THE CITADEL: A VIEW FROM THE TOP

Since 1749, when it was founded to counter the French threat at the Fortress of Louisbourg, Halifax has prospered during conflict and borne the brunt of peace. And almost from the beginning, there has been a fortress atop Citadel Hill to watch over the town's fortunes. Edward Cornwallis, the first Governor of the new colony, recognized the strategic importance of the site; he built one of his five stockaded forts on the hill. A second fortification was built during the American Revolution to stave off the invasion that never came. Prince Edward, the Duke of Kent (eventually, father of Queen Victoria), greatly expanded the Citadel during his tenure as commander of the garrison in the 1790s (in order to do this, he levelled the hill by cutting off its top). The present

fortification, the fourth on this site, was built in the wake of the War of 1812, when the threat of an American invasion was once again palpable. The Citadel's military function has long since been exhausted. Instead,

it has become the most visited national historic site in Canada — a treasured legacy from colonial times.

It was the Duke of Wellington, fresh from his defeat of Napoleon at Waterloo in 1815, who pushed for the construction of a fourth fortress on Citadel Hill. The Americans had shown their true colours during the War of 1812 and with the enemy so close at hand the Iron Duke felt it necessary to protect Halifax's naval dockyard from a land attack. Ironically, the initial plans for the new fortress were drawn up by Colonel James Arnold (the Americans had cause to remember his father, Benedict).

The construction of the fortress was a major local industry for more than 30 years. Whether the effort was necessary is open to debate. No attack came. The Citadel's smooth-bore cannon were never shot in anger. And, shortly after its completion in 1856, the introduction of long range, rifled naval guns downgraded its strategic importance.

The fortress on Citadel Hill has been put to various uses in this century. During the First World War, prisoners from the German merchant marine were kept here. Several escaped using kitchen knives, hangers, and blankets — proof positive that, at the very least, the Citadel walls could be breached from the inside out. One prisoner named Bronstein spent

MIDDLE: SOUTH RAVELIN

BOTTOM: POWDER MAGAZINE

several weeks here in 1917 while officials checked out some suspicious travel documents. The Russian Government secured his release and Bronstein, who called himself Leon Trotsky, went on to his place in history.

For much of the Second World War, the Citadel served as temporary barracks for troops going overseas (more than 17,000 ships left in convoy from Halifax Harbour during the war). It was also the centre of anti-aircraft operations in Halifax.

With peace, came neglect. The Citadel languished until it was declared a national historic site in 1951. Today, it is the city's major tourist attraction, where meticulously reconstructed fortifications and Parks Canada staff combine to bring one of Canada's most significant defence works back to life.

You can approach the Citadel from any point of the compass, but there are steps leading up to the fortification from the top of George Street. This route takes you past the **Old Town Clock** which has marked the time at the base

BELOW: OLD TOWN CLOCK

RIGHT: UNDER THE RAMPARTS OF THE CITADEL ENTRANCE

BELOW: THE 78TH HIGHLANDERS

BOTTOM: OLD TOWN CLOCK

of Citadel Hill since 1803. The clock was a gift to the city from Prince Edward. Unperturbed by such cataclysmic events as the Halifax Explosion in 1917, the clock has been restored to ensure that it will remain, in the words of Joseph Howe, "a good example to all the idle chaps in town".

Once inside the walls of the Citadel, you can arrange for a first-rate guided tour in either French or English. The fort's military routines are carried out as they were in 1869-71. Students take on the roles of soldiers from the 78th Highlanders and the Royal Artillery, along with sailors of the

Naval Brigade. They drill according to instructions laid out in 1860s manuals. There are piping demonstrations.

One of the most popular activities is the firing of the noon gun, which can be heard daily throughout downtown Halifax.

Your guide will take you inside the barrel-vaulted casemates that once housed the troops, and on to the musket galleries and ravelins, designed to cause trepidation among the attackers who never came. Ask about the fort's visual telegraph system. Signal flags above the ramparts once told civilians what merchant ships were in the harbour. They were also used to alert the other harbour fortifications of the movements of friendly and enemy warships. At one time, it was thought that a series of signalling stations could be used to reach as far as Quebec! After your tour, you may want to view the exhibits on communications, the four Citadels, and the

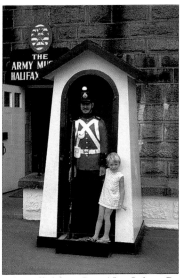

engineering and construction of the fourth Citadel. "The Tides of History", a 40-minute audio visual presentation, provides a dramatic look at Halifax's military history. The on-site **Army Museum** has an extensive collection of guns and military dress. There is also a gift shop. Although the Citadel grounds are open year round, the site is only staffed from June 15 to Labour Day, between 9am-6pm. Admission is charged.

Do not leave the fort before using its commanding views to familiarize yourself with the city's geography. Look down at the harbour slope where surveyor Charles Morris laid out the streets of the new garrison town in 1749. The rock in the middle of the harbour is George's Island, once an important part of the Halifax defence complex; likewise McNab's Island, which lies further out the harbour on the Dartmouth side. The Northwest Arm, which forms the western boundary of the Halifax Peninsula, is to the southwest of the fort. In the distance, a Martello tower at York Redoubt used to guard the entrance to the harbour. You can see the Halifax Common from the northwest battlements of the Citadel. The Common was originally set aside as pasture land. Because no

ABOVE: TUNIC AND TOOLS OF THE ROYAL ARTILLERY

BELOW: SIGNAL MASTS REVEALED SHIP MOVEMENTS

BOTTOM: NINETEENTH CENTURY BARRACKS

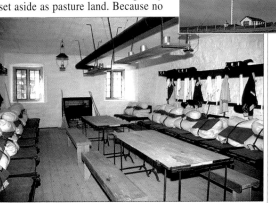

ABOVE: THE GUARD ROOM

structures were allowed to interfere with the line of fire from the fortresses atop Citadel Hill, the Common remained a green space. Today, it is a favourite recreational area for city residents.

With this picture of Halifax in mind, you should have no problem orienting yourself on the walking tours that follow. Enjoy the city!

DOWNTOWN HALIFAX

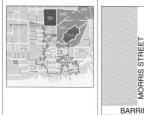

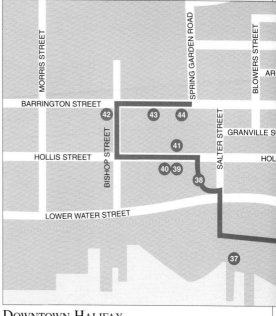

DOWNTOWN HALIFAX

This tour takes you along the harbour slope of Citadel Hill, the heart of Old Halifax. Here, in the summer of 1749, surveyor Charles Morris and engineer John Brewse laid out the new garrison town in a rectangular grid that marched up the hill from the water. Street names like Barrington, Argyle, Sackville, Grafton, George, and Granville pay tribute to patrons and leading British statesmen of the day. Many would have been disappointed by the modest town that grew out of the ambitious plan conceived in London. But Halifax has not suffered the loss of the lavish equestrian statue of George II intended for the Grand Parade — nor many of the other flourishes that were planned.

Halifax survived and eventually prospered under the watchful eye of the Citadel. This tour tells much of the story. Contrast the sturdy pioneer charm of St. Paul's Anglican Church (the town's original building) with the Georgian refinement of Province House (completed in 1819). Along the waterfront at Historic Properties, forests of spars once crowded warehouses brimming with the booty of privateers. At a discreet distance from the raucous waterfront, goldsmiths, furriers, haberdashers, and china merchants filled the fashionable shops that lined Granville Street. By the end of the 19th century, a new tram car was only the most visible symbol of the bustling commercial thoroughfare that was Barrington Street.

ST. PAUL'S

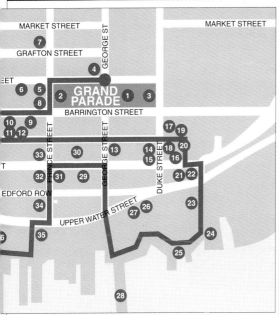

Architecturally, the city's downtown core remained remarkably intact until the 1960s, when many historic buildings were replaced by office towers. The earlier removal of the Eaton's Department Store, once the stalwart among Canadian retailers, to a suburban mall, was a serious blow to the downtown. Other retailers followed (city council is still looking for ways to get them back). Buildings of architectural significance were vacated and slated for demolition. But preservationists won important battles — beginning with the conservation of seven waterfront warehouses (now "Historic Properties") in the face of plans for a new expressway. Today many buildings are listed as Heritage Properties; long stretches of both Barrington and Granville streets look like they did in the 19th century. At several points along your walk you will be struck by the clash of modern steel and glass with Georgian slate and sandstone, evidence of battles lost and won.

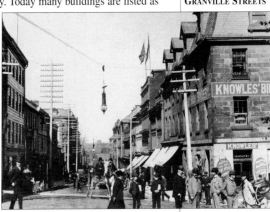

Begin your tour at the **Grand Parade (1)**, the centre of Old Halifax. At the south end of the square, **St. Paul's Anglican Church (2)**, completed in 1750, is the oldest Protestant church in Canada and Halifax's first building. St. Paul's was patterned on James Gibbs's design for Marybone Chapel (now, St. Peter's Vere Street), in London. Gibbs apprenticed with Christopher Wren, and his work includes the beautiful St. Martin-in-the-Fields in

Trafalgar Square. The unadorned classical features and baroque steeple are typical of his designs. The oak frame and pine timbers of the church were prefabricated in Boston and shipped to Halifax along with lanterns for the town's first streetlights.

Inside, St. Paul's has undergone many changes including the addition of galleries and stained glass — Victorian touches that mask the church's colonial

INTERIOR OF ST. PAUL'S

roots. But the rough hewn box pews, reminiscent of a New England Meeting House, recall the time when the Church of England shared St. Paul's with its Dissenting brethren. Sermons preached in Mi'kmaq and German were common in those early years. Still, beneath the floor of the church dubbed the "Westminster Abbey of the New World" are the burial vaults of bishops, governors and generals. St. Paul's is opened year round and you can reflect on the church's colourful past during Sunday services at 8:30am, 10:30am and 7:30pm.

When you leave St. Paul's, look across the square to **City Hall (3)**, dwarfed somewhat by the office towers in the background. This attractive Victorian building, with its distinctive clock tower and gabled dormers, was designed by Dartmouth architect, Edward Elliot. It took years of wrangling before officials of Dalhousie University agreed to part with the plot of land where City Hall now stands. Some say that the deal still allows Dalhousie students to drive horse drawn carts through the Grand Parade!

LOOKING ACROSS THE GRAND PARADE

RIGHT: CITY HALL

During a servicemen's riot in 1918, Halifax police were holed up in the basement of City Hall for hours while the building was pelted with bricks hurled by soldiers, sailors, and sundry others who bore the police a grudge. The riot was not quelled until a British cruiser landed a column of armed sailors and marines.

Take the steps leading up to Argyle Street from the Grand Parade. The building which now houses the **Five Fishermen Restaurant (4)** was once home to the Victoria School of Art and Design. The driving force behind the school was Anna Leonowens, the governess immortalized in the Rodgers and Hammerstein musical *The King and I*, who took a keen interest in the local artistic community upon her arrival in Halifax with her daughter and son-in-law in 1876. Today, her legacy lives on in the classrooms and studios of the Nova Scotia College of Art and Design on Granville Street.

CITY HALL'S
CENTRAL PORTICO

Now turn left on Argyle Street. As you pass by St. Paul's, look for the profile of the vicar who died in the Halifax Explosion of 1917; some say he can still be seen in one of the upper windows.

Continue along Argyle to the corner of Prince Street. The core of the **Carleton Hotel (5)** was once the home of Richard Bulkeley (it was Bulkeley who was sent to Boston to fetch the frame and timbers for St. Paul's). He was also judge of the Vice-Admiralty Court, and the disposition of privateers' booty took place in the drawing room of his home. It is thought that some of the stone used to construct the original building came from the French Fortress of Louisbourg, following its demolition by British

sappers in 1760. The Carleton Hotel itself has narrowly escaped demolition as developers and heritage conservationists try and decide its future.

You are now within striking

distance of two Halifax institutions, the **Seahorse Tavern (6)** (just ahead on Argyle Street) and the **Midtown Tavern (7)**, at the corner of Prince and Grafton streets. Almost empty by day, the Seahorse's eclectic clientele, ranging from bikers to the sons and daughters of wealthy South End families, pack the tavern in the evening. Sturdy fare, draught beer and sports talk characterize busy lunches and dinners at the Midtown. The Alexander Keith's Society, united by their love of Halifax's legendary brewer and his beer, meets here on Friday afternoons.

DOWN GEORGE STREET TO THE HARBOUR

Turn left on Prince Street and walk down the hill to Barrington Street. The tour will take you to the right, along Barrington as far as Sackville Street; if you are especially interested in Victorian commercial buildings then you should certainly continue along Barrington toward Spring Garden Road to see the rest of the city's most architecturally significant streetscape. Then trace your steps to rejoin the tour at Sackville Street.

Barrington Street was important from the beginning. Close to the Grand Parade, it was a conduit for news and gossip. The town's elite took Sunday constitutionals

BARRINGTON STREET IN THE HIGH VICTORIAN ERA

RIGHT: SHOP FRONTS ON BARRINGTON STREET

BELOW: WRIGHT BUILDING, BARRINGTON STREET

along the south section of Barrington (then, Pleasant Street) to Point Pleasant. In the earliest years, they were often escorted by British redcoats — necessary protection from Mi'kmaq raiding parties. Commercially, Barrington was overshadowed by the streets below it until the late 19th century when a flurry of building activity made it bustle. Many of these new buildings were of steel beam construction, a new technology that emerged in the wake of the Chicago fire of 1871. The walls of these Chicago-style structures were not load-bearing so that they were often built high with lots of windows and decorative arches (the style eventually gave rise to modern skyscrapers).

Cross to the harbour side of Barrington and look back at the **Wright Building (8)** (nos. 1672-4). George Wright, whose entrepreneurial firsts included "Wright's World Directory" (distributed worldwide by Lloyd's), commissioned this Chicago-style building in 1896. Its ultramodern aspect attracted Guglielmo Marconi, inventor of the wireless, who set up shop here for four years. Ironically, Wright, who had tied his faith and fortune to progress, was one of 33 millionaires to go down with the *Titanic* in 1912.

Still at the corner of Prince and Barrington streets is the **Nova Scotia Centre for Craft and Design (9)**. The centre's Mary E. Black Gallery displays the work of many of the province's best craftspeople and designers. There are studios where you can see weaving, woodworking, and jewellery-making in progress. The centre will also provide information that will lead you to the open studios of craftspeople and visual artists throughout Nova Scotia.

Back outside, continue along Barrington to Sackville Street. Along the way, you will see elegant commercial buildings that once housed the mainstays of Barrington Street's retail sector. Setbacks like the departure of Colwell Bros. clothing store after 75 years from the beautiful, Italianate **Colwell Building (10)** (no. 1673) have been hard to recover from.

Turn down Sackville, then left onto Granville Street. **The Book Room (11)**, established in 1839, is Canada's oldest bookstore and Halifax's largest. Ideal for browsing, the store has a wide selection of regional books. Ask about The Book Room's mail order service.

Further along, on your right, is the back of Province House, the zenith of Georgian architecture in the city (later, the tour will take you inside). The statue you see in the back garden is Joseph Howe, a Nova Scotian folk hero. In 1835, disgruntled magistrates brought a criminal libel charge against Howe after his newspaper, the *Nova Scotian*, printed a letter charging them with mismanagement. In an eloquent six-hour oration, Howe successfully defended himself, his paper, and freedom of speech from the charges, whereupon he was borne triumphantly from the Court Room (now the Legislative Library) of Province House upon the shoulders of a throng of admirers. Thus began a celebrated political career and a genuine folk legend.

A little further along on your left at 1700 Granville is the **Nova Scotia Government Bookstore (12)**. If you plan to spend part of your Nova Scotia holiday outdoors, then government publications and maps available at the store will assist with activities like canoeing and hiking.

THE WORK OF NOVA SCOTIA ARTISANS ON DISPLAY AT THE CENTRE FOR CRAFT AND DESIGN

STATUE OF JOSEPH HOWE AT PROVINCE HOUSE

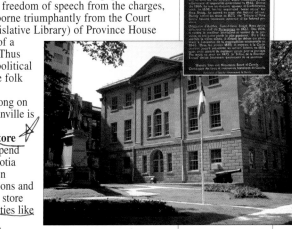

29

PROVINCE HOUSE

Continue north on Granville, past the old bank buildings that were once important measures of worth. The old **Bank of Commerce Building (13)** at the northeast corner of Granville and George streets, with its massive Greek Temple style pillars, inspired confidence among clients. So did the elegant Italianate **Merchants' Bank of Canada Building (14)**, further along at the southeast corner of Duke and Granville. Now, most Halifax banks look down on their former premises

from the office towers that crowd this part of downtown (a notable exception, the Bank of Nova Scotia still occupies its distinctive Hollis Street premises).

Around the corner from the old Merchants' Bank on

J.J. ROSSY'S, GRANVILLE STREET

Duke Street, Nova Scotia's foremost restaurateur "Fat Frank" Metzger offers fine city dining at **Trouter's Grill (15)**.

The section of Granville Street that lies ahead was restored as part of the Historic Properties project that began in the 1960s (it is now closed to traffic). In September 1859, fire laid to waste this stretch of Granville. The superb streetscape that arose from this devastation was designed by William Thomas &

Sons of Toronto (their other designs include the Old Court House on Spring Garden Road and St. Matthew's Church on Barrington Street). Elaborate windows and arches are what jump out at you. Not everyone approved of these extravagances. Nineteenth century Halifax historian T.B. Akins remarked: "The whole of this part of Granville

THE PROMENADE, GRANVILLE STREET

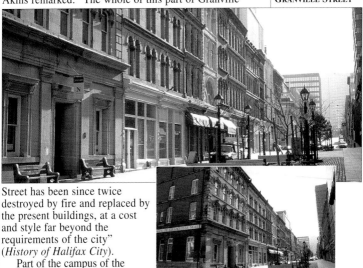

Street has been since twice destroyed by fire and replaced by the present buildings, at a cost and style far beyond the requirements of the city" (*History of Halifax City*).

Part of the campus of the **Nova Scotia College of Art and Design (16)** is located on the east side of the street. Here, you can see the avant garde work of NSCAD students on display at the Anna Leonowens Gallery.

Barrington Place (17) is on Granville Street's west side. In 1978, the original façade was dismantled, the stones numbered, then painstakingly reassembled to reinforce the harbour side wall of the Delta Barrington Hotel. Such care was rewarded. Exposed cobblestones and the Victorian water trough where horses once slaked their thirst round out the scene, making this one of the most agreeable places in downtown Halifax.

You can slake your thirst at pubs like the **Split Crow (18)** and **Peddler's (19)**. The Split Crow offers nightly entertainment — usually with a Celtic flair. The Saturday matinees at Peddler's have been popular for years. Both pubs have outdoor patios (though these are often crowded) where you can sip a draught beer while admiring the impressive surroundings.

PEDDLER'S PUB

After refreshment, you may want to do some shopping. There are several fine shops in **Barrington Place**. Upstairs, Colwell Bros. has been sprucing up Haligonians with its quality clothing since 1891. Daskalides sells luscious Belgian chocolates. Downstairs, even non-smokers will find it hard to resist the redolent tobacco smells of MacDonald Tobacco and Gifts. MacDonald's fills orders from discriminating pipe and cigar smokers worldwide. Also on this level, the craft division of the Micmac Heritage Gallery sells beautiful handmade baskets, leather goods, and jewellery. The gallery itself displays Native fine art from across Canada.

Cross the street, and walk through the entrance to the **Shops of Granville Mall (20)**, where you can see exposed brick from the old alley that was enclosed as part of the restoration. Here, Port of Wines is a specialty shop with a good selection of imported wines and spirits. Nova Scotia Images features the photographs of Maurice Crosby. Like Nova Scotia's most famous photographer, Wallace MacAskill, Crosby's favourite subject is the sea. Traditional Maritime scenes abound — fish shacks, yellow-hulled dories, and more (prints are reasonably priced).

Exit the Shops of Granville Mall onto Hollis Street. **Nemo's Restaurant (21)** offers Provençale and northern Italian cuisine in intimate surroundings. Turn left toward the **Morse's Tea Building (22)**, where, earlier this century, tasters trained on the tea plantations of India assisted J.E. Morse and Company in blending their India and China teas for worldwide export. Tea tasting is not part of the curriculum at NSCAD, which now occupies the building.

MORSE'S TEA BUILDING

RIGHT: PRIVATEERS' WAREHOUSE

Walk around the Morse Building and cross the street to see the seven waterfront warehouses that are the core of the **Historic Properties (23)** development. The survival of these superb examples of Georgian industrial architecture was a near thing. One building actually withstood a

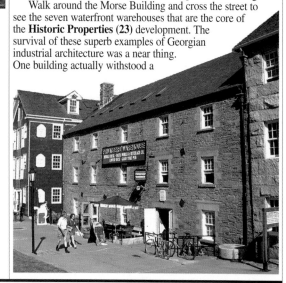

blow from the wrecking ball before plans for a waterfront expressway were abandoned. After a long struggle, Parks Canada designated these buildings a National Historic Site.

Above the Water Street entrance of the building directly across from Morse's, you can see the word "Bank" carved into the sandstone. The official name of this bank, established in 1825, was the Halifax Banking Company, but everybody called it Collins Bank. And Enos Collins probably liked it that way. The one-time schooner captain from Liverpool, Nova Scotia, grew to be one of the richest men in British North America.

A large part of Collins' fortune came from legalized privateering raids off the New England coast during the War of 1812. His *Liverpool Packet* terrorized merchant shipping. The privateers' booty was stored in a warehouse to the rear of the bank (now "Privateers' Warehouse"). Built in 1813, this is the oldest building of the group. Booty from the U.S. frigate *Chesapeake* was kept here after its capture outside Boston harbour by the *Shannon* in 1813. (The last words of the *Chesapeake's* captain — "Don't give up the ship!" — remain the motto of the U.S. Navy.)

TRADITIONAL QUILTS AT SUTTLES AND SEAWINDS

Before the wharf was reconstructed and a sea-wall built, the wooden buildings nearest the water had loose floorboards that would float freely during very high tides, to be easily replaced later. Some say this also allowed small craft to sail under the warehouses at low tide and unload illicit cargoes in the dead of night.

Today, you will find a variety of shops and services in these waterfront warehouses. The Pickford and Black building with its Carpenter Shop, and two old inns, Pontac House and Anchorage House, are now under one roof, and the site of an attractive mall. The distinctive line of clothing at Suttles & Seawinds, a local company, has won international acclaim. Many of the colourful designs were inspired by traditional quilts. At the Windsor Wear Mill Merchant, you will find some of

the best long underwear anywhere (those who prefer Truro-made Stanfield's may disagree). Windsor Wear makes quality T-shirts and sweatshirts as well.

The Lower Deck Good Time Pub in Privateers' Warehouse features local entertainment with plenty of audience participation. Long tables resembling mead benches are scarred where empty draught glasses have been used to pound out lively Celtic rhythms. Not the place for a quiet drink, but ideal for a boisterous evening full of atmosphere. Upstairs, in calmer surroundings, the Upper Deck prepares some of the city's best seafood dishes. Try and get a table with a harbour view. Across the way at the water's edge, Salty's offers more casual dining with a view of the harbour practically guaranteed.

Just across the street on the other side of Lower Water Street are two more enjoyable dining spots.

BLUENOSE II AT **HISTORIC PROPERTIES**

O'Carroll's is a prime lunching spot for Halifax's business crowd; you can spot corporate presidents and directors while enjoying pleasant surroundings and good food. Next door is Sweet Basil's, where the chef specializes in lighter, more contemporary cooking and fine desserts.

Close by, at the Old Red Store (another property that came under the control of Enos Collins), the Province operates a full-service **Visitor Information Centre (24)**. If you plan on a harbour tour or a guided walking tour, then the centre can help. Knowledgeable staff will answer any other questions you have about your stay in Halifax and assist with arrangements, including accommodation, for the rest of your Nova Scotian holiday.

As you leave the Visitor Information Centre to walk along the waterfront, keep an eye out for the *Bluenose II*, which is often docked beside the Old Red Store. Built in 1963, this replica of the world's most famous schooner (depicted on the Canadian dime), underwent an extensive refit to make it seaworthy for the G-7 Summit in Halifax in 1995. It is expected that *Bluenose II* will continue its distinguished service as a Nova Scotian ambassador for years to come.

TOP LEFT: HALIFAX-DARTMOUTH FERRY

Walk south along the waterfront to the **Halifax-Dartmouth Ferry Terminal (25)** (Tour 5). In service since 1752, the passenger ferry is still one of the best ways to see the Halifax and Dartmouth waterfronts, and easily the cheapest (a one-way trip costs $1.00). Go upstairs to the rooftop terrace for a great view of the city's most valuable resource, its harbour.

FISHERMAN'S MARKET

Adjoining the ferry terminal on Lower Water Street is **Perks (26)**, a cheerful and enjoyable locally owned espresso bar and coffee shop. Along with your coffee you can pick from an array of sandwiches, croissants, muffins and cookies. Across from Perks is the **Fisherman's Market (27)**, where you can buy a variety of fresh fish and shellfish including lobsters packed in special containers for your flight home.

Halifax Harbour is one of the world's best, extending inland about 16 kilometres (10 mi.) from its seaward approaches, through The Narrows spanned by the two bridges connecting Halifax and Dartmouth, and into the Bedford Basin. From your perch atop the Ferry Terminal, you might spy navy frigates, submarines, container ships, general cargo ships,

or luxury yachts. To your left is the Angus L. Macdonald Bridge — beyond it, the newer A. Murray MacKay Bridge. On your right is George's Island with its old fortification and lighthouse. Further out the harbour is McNab's Island, where mutineers were hung in chains on Mauger's Beach during the Napoleonic Wars.

You can also look down on **Cable Wharf (28)**, the former home of the Great Western Union cable ships that laid out and maintained the trans-Atlantic telegraph and telephone cables. Today, a variety of harbour tours and private charters dock here (there is also a ferry service to McNab's Island). Later, you may want to take a tour that includes historical

HALIFAX TOWN CRIER

ART GALLERY OF
NOVA SCOTIA

commentary, whale-watching, or an on-board meal. There are also "party" cruises. Or you might be interested in a deep-sea fishing charter. Get out on the water if you can; it's a great way to see the city.

Continue along the terrace, past the Law Courts, and across the pedway. Notice the historic sandstone buildings alongside the steel and glass of modern office towers. At the end of the pedway, cross George Street to Bedford Row. Take the stairs on your right to get to Cheapside, once the site of an open-air market. You have arrived at the **Art Gallery of Nova Scotia (29)**. Completed in 1868, this beautiful Italianate structure was built to provide offices in Halifax for the new Canadian government. You only have to look to the 12-foot statue of Britannia seated atop the building to realize that England still held a place in the hearts of Haligonians on the eve of Confederation.

Inside, the gallery's extensive collection features Canadian, British, and European works, but the real treasures come from local artists. The collection of folk art on the mezzanine level is outstanding. The Gallery Shop sells handcrafted work of the highest quality — folk art, jewellery, pottery, and glass. There is also a wide selection of postcards, notecards,

PROVINCE HOUSE

RIGHT: TWO VIEWS OF THE ASSEMBLY CHAMBER

and handmade cards by Nova Scotian artists.

When you leave the Art Gallery, cross Cheapside to Hollis Street, where you will see the well-composed, classical features of **Province House (30)**, completed in 1819. The government had had to wait for its new home until

after Governor and Lady Wentworth were properly situated in their lavish new residence (more on the Wentworths and Government House later). Province House was worth waiting for. During an 1842 visit to Halifax, Charles Dickens described it as a "gem of Georgian architecture." The Palladian-style building really is beautiful — remarkably so, given that it was designed by John Merrick, a local paint contractor (the Government was wary of professional architects after the exorbitant cost of Government House).

BELOW RIGHT: HANGING STAIRCASE IN THE LEGISLATIVE LIBRARY

Tour guides are always on hand to take you through the interior of Province House. The splendid Red Chamber, with its tall windows and ornate plasterwork, has changed little since the building's earliest days. The oak table you see came from the *Beaufort*, the ship that brought Edward Cornwallis here in June of 1749. Since the Upper House of the provincial parliament was abolished in

1928, this room has been used mostly for ceremonial functions (Province House administrators are constantly turning down requests to hold wedding receptions here).

The Legislative Library, once the courtroom where Joseph Howe made his triumphant speech, is also magnificent. The hanging staircases and three-sided balcony were added when the room was converted to a library in 1862. So were the eight alcoves — complete with intricate, wrought-iron mayflowers (Nova Scotia's provincial flower). Members who seek refuge from the strife of the Legislative Assembly must find the library an oasis.

The Nova Scotia Legislature has met in the Assembly Chamber every year since 1819. Dickens saw the Assembly

in session in 1842, wryly remarking that it was like looking at the House of Commons at Westminster through the wrong end of a telescope. Certainly the partisanship would have been familiar to him. Even the portraits of two prominent statesmen, Charles Tupper (a Conservative) and William Fielding (a Liberal), switch sides of the Assembly Chamber following a change of government!

Of course, there is a wealth of lore within the walls of Province House. Before leaving, look for the headless eagles over the door of the South Committee Room. Apparently, with anti-American sentiment running high during the Fenian scare of the 1840s, one Member took it upon himself to whack the heads off the accursed eagles with his cane. It is not known whether he ever discovered that the eagles were, in fact, falcons.

Leave the way you came and continue south along Hollis Street (with the traffic). On your left is the **Bank of Nova Scotia (31)**, an impressive 1930s building in the Art Deco style. Further along, at the southeast corner of Hollis and

DETAILS AT THE BANK OF NOVA SCOTIA

BELOW: FOUNDERS' SQUARE

THE HALIFAX CLUB

RIGHT: MCKELVIE'S RESTAURANT

MARITIME MUSEUM OF THE ATLANTIC

Prince, is **Founders' Square (32)**. In the late 19th century when Halifax boomed, 14 newspapers were published within the walls that now form part of this modern office complex.

The ornate Italianate building on the other side of Hollis Street is home to the **Halifax Club (33)**, formerly a Victorian gentlemen's club replete with overstuffed chairs and attentive service. The atmosphere is unchanged, but the club now has both male and female members.

Turn left down Prince Street. At Bedford Row, **McKelvie's Restaurant (34)** now occupies the old No. 6 Fire Hall. The broad arches you see at the front of the building were once doors where horse-drawn fire engines came and went. The restaurant features imaginatively prepared seafood.

At the bottom of Prince, cross Lower Water Street. On your right, the **Maritime Museum of the Atlantic (35)** tells much of Halifax's seafaring story. Inside, there are exhibits on the Halifax Explosion, shipwrecks and lifesaving, the

Titanic, the Navy, steamships, and sailing ships. The old William Robertson & Son ship chandlery has been restored. And you will also find lots of boats — about 70 in all — from Mi'kmaq

birchbark canoes to a Royal Barge once used by Queen Victoria.

There are many stories to go along with the museum's artifacts. There's the Swedish greaser aboard the ill-fated *Imo* (one of the two ships involved in the collision that resulted in the Halifax Explosion of 1917) who was informed of his own death by the Swedish Consul in New York a year later. And the Halifax harbour pilot who was stranded aboard

the luxurious *Aquitania* during a storm and ended up going all the way to New York. For his troubles, the crew of the *Aquitania* presented him with a tea service, now on display at the museum.

Exit at the rear, to the museum's wharf, where the *Acadia* is docked. You are invited aboard this hydrographic vessel, which spent more than five decades surveying waters from the Bay of Fundy to Hudson Bay. Afterwards, walk to the end of the wharf to conduct your own survey of the harbour. There are often pleasure craft berthed at the adjacent wharves during the summer months.

Nearby is the *HMCS Sackville,* a World War II convoy escort corvette which has been restored as a memorial to

ABOVE: THE WILLIAM ROBERTSON & SON CHANDLERY

LEFT: *C.S.S. ACADIA*

those who served in the Canadian Navy. An interpretation centre tells the story of the Battle of the Atlantic.

Continue south along the waterside boardwalk, past **Sackville Landing (36)**, to a working stretch of shoreline. From here, the pilot boat is dispatched to guide large ships in and out of the harbour. A little further along, the massive tugboats of **Eastern Canada Towing (37)** are docked. These floating engines were the inspiration for the popular children's television program "Theodore Tugboat". There are several fine vantage points from which to view the harbour along here; the "ships in the harbour" displays on the boardwalk will help you to identify all kinds of shipping.

At the end of the boardwalk turn right onto Salter Street, between the vast parking lots that await someone's better idea. Just ahead to the left is **Alexander Keith's Brewery (38)**. In 1837, the Scottish-born brewer decided to expand his Lower Water

ALEXANDER KEITH'S BREWERY

Street premises. With the help of high rum prices (slave labour had been abolished in the West Indies), Keith's business flourished within the imposing ironstone walls of the new brewery. Although the Keith interests were bought out by the Oland family shortly after the First World War, Alexander Keith's India Pale Ale (now brewed by Labatt)

remains the favourite beer of Nova Scotians.

Today, the restored Brewery is frequently held up as an example of what can be achieved by preservation-minded developers. Its red brick interior, with gothic windows and arches, provides a comfortable setting for restaurants and offices. For memorable Italian cuisine in a unique setting, make dinner reservations at da Maurizio, one of the city's best restaurants. The Brewery also hosts a farmers' market where local crafts, baked goods and produce are available. The market is open Saturday mornings year round, and Friday mornings during summer. To leave the Brewery, look for the sign marked "Bottling Plant" in the central courtyard, which will direct you to the Hollis Street exit.

A left turn onto Hollis takes you past several historic houses. You only have to look at the lavish Italianate mansion at 1475 Hollis to see how good the beer business was to Alexander Keith. **Keith Hall (39)** was built in 1863 when Alexander's fortune was already made, but he still took a keen interest in his business (the house and brewery were connected by a tunnel). Next door is

ABOVE TOP: KEITH HALL

BENJAMIN WIER HOUSE

RIGHT: OLD PRESBYTERIAN MANSE

another Italianate building, **Benjamin Wier House (40)**, built around the same time as Keith Hall. Across the street is **Black-Binney House (41)**. John Black built the house in 1819 with money made from privateering. A later occupant, the Right Reverend Hibbert Binney, attained the singular distinction of marrying while holding the office of bishop.

The long stone wall that follows Black-Binney House protects the garden of Government House (built to face Hollis Street, the back of Government House has since become its front). Turn right onto Bishop Street. During the 1880s, the old **Presbyterian Manse (42)** at the corner of Barrington and Bishop Streets was the temporary home of Dalhousie student Lucy Maud Montgomery, who went on to write *Anne of Green Gables*.

A right turn onto Barrington Street takes you to the front (once the back) of **Government House (43)**, home of the

ENTRANCE TO GOVERNMENT HOUSE

Lieutenant-Governor. The house was built for John and Frances Wentworth, well-connected New Hampshire Loyalists, who took Halifax by storm during the late 18th century. Frances, especially, created a sensation with her Royal liaisons. Prince William

frequented her bedchamber during visits to Halifax in the 1780s. Her behaviour scandalized Halifax Society. But it did not hurt John's political aspirations. He became Lieutenant-Governor in 1792. He and Frances, bolstered by their intimate alliance with royalty, then set to work upgrading their accommodation.

The cornerstone of Government House was laid in September of 1800. The handsome Georgian building in the Palladian style exceeded cost estimates and expectations. It was grandeur on a scale that prompted a later Lieutenant-Governor to seek a pay raise upon viewing his new home. Unfortunately for the Wentworths, they were pensioned off to their Bedford Basin lodge shortly after Government House was completed in 1807.

Normally off-limits to the public, the Lieutenant-Governor continues a long-standing tradition of hosting a New Year's Day levee, when everyone is invited inside Government House for a look (and a glass of sherry).

Continue along Barrington Street to **St. Matthew's Church (44)** (yet another Halifax building designed by the Toronto firm of William Thomas & Sons). You are now at the foot of Spring Garden Road and the end of this tour.

ST. MATTHEW'S CHURCH

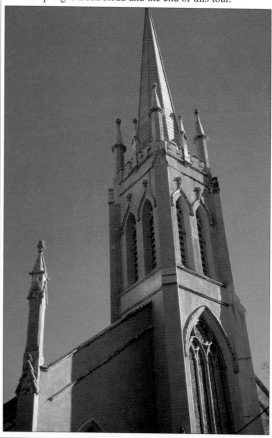

SPRING GARDEN ROAD

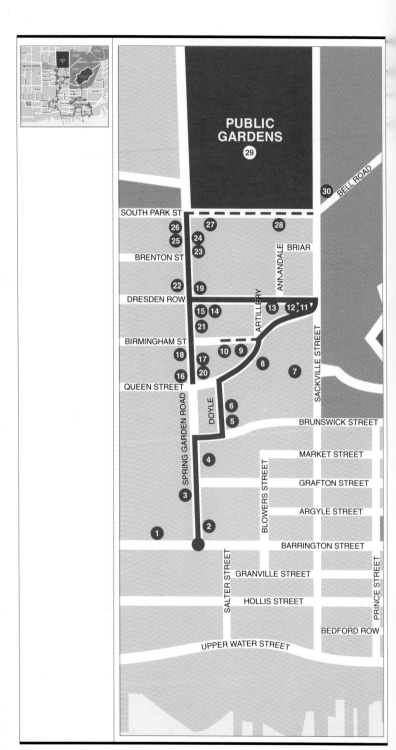

SPRING GARDEN ROAD

ABOVE: THE PUBLIC
GARDENS

Spring Garden Road, dubbed "the most prettily named downtown street in Canada" by Nova Scotian writer Harry Bruce, started out as a mud track to the governor's garden (now site of the Old Court House) shortly after the founding of Halifax. Where the Halifax City Regional Library now stands, a poorhouse once overlooked shallow paupers' graves. But it was not long before the street was living up to the fashionable name given it by nostalgic Londoners. By the early 1800s, Prince Edward's "Bellevue" mansion was among the large estates that lined Spring Garden Road.

Today, the city's best shops, restaurants and cafés help sustain Spring Garden Road's fashionable tone. Look for fine jewellery, designer clothing and distinctive gifts — all within the four Spring Garden blocks bounded by Queen and South Park streets.

Start your tour at the **Old Burying Ground (1)** (St. Paul's Cemetery), across Barrington Street from Government House,

WELSFORD-PARKER MONUMENT

RIGHT: ST. MARY'S BASILICA FROM THE OLD BURYING GROUND

at the foot of Spring Garden Road. Now a national historic site, St. Paul's was the town's original cemetery and a busy place during those early years. Thomas Raddall, Nova Scotia's favourite novelist and a prolific amateur historian, described the macabre drama played out here during the winter of 1749-50: "We may picture the rum-primed gravediggers, the shivering guard of redcoats watching the forest, the perfunctory parsons, the unwilling mourners, the pine coffins with their carved initials, and the air of gloom over all" (*Halifax: Warden of the North*).

Dated 1754, the oldest extant marker belongs to John Connor, the original operator of the Halifax-Dartmouth ferry. Keep an eye out for the strangely demonic lion's head that gazes down from the Welsford-Parker Monument, at the cemetery gates. This is North America's only memorial to the Crimean War. The Old Burying Ground is open from 9am to 5pm daily during the summer; you can pick up maps and information on stones at St. Paul's Anglican Church (Tour 2).

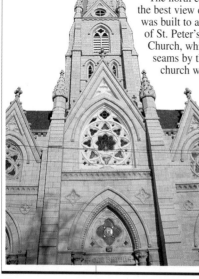

The north end of the Old Burying Ground affords the best view of **St. Mary's Basilica (2)**. St. Mary's was built to accommodate the growing congregation of St. Peter's, the town's original Roman Catholic Church, which was close to bursting its wooden seams by the time the cornerstone of the new church was laid in 1820. St. Peter's was eventually dismantled and floated across the harbour where it rose again to serve as Dartmouth's first Roman Catholic church. St. Mary's was under the spiritual and architectural direction of the first Roman Catholic Bishop of Nova Scotia, Edmund Burke. Burke's Georgian Gothic revival style cathedral was built of ironstone (schistose slate) quarried from across the Northwest Arm — the stone of choice for many Halifax buildings of the period. During the 1860s the elaborate Victorian façade and soaring 189-foot high spire were added. As you leave the cemetery and start walking up Spring Garden Road, look back to see the startling contrast of the Basilica's white granite façade with its grey-black ironstone walls.

Next you will come to the **Old Court House (3)**. The centre section of this imposing neo-classical structure was built in 1860 by the Toronto firm William Thomas and Sons (they also designed St. Matthew's Church on Barrington Street). You need not go inside to find the stern face of Justice — just look to the lion and human heads above the entrance. They, along with massive Tuscan columns, provide a silent admonition to those about to have their cases heard in provincial court.

The **Halifax City Regional Library (4)** is across the street. The Grand Parade may be the city's official public square (Tour 2), but the little park in front of the library is

where everyone hangs out. Business people and secretaries, street people and buskers, students and seniors, starlings and pigeons, all come here — especially at lunchtime. The two chip wagons operated by Bud the Spud and brother Bill have been waylaying healthy-minded Haligonians for years. The fries are delicious! Amidst the bustle broods a statue of Winston Churchill, oblivious to it all.

Now, turn right off Spring Garden Road onto Brunswick Street. The **Halifax Folklore Centre (5)** provides the city's best introduction to the traditional music of Nova Scotia. The centre stocks recordings by the province's finest musicians (look for the rousing Cape Breton fiddle tunes of sensational performers Natalie MacMaster and Ashley MacIsaac). You can see the pervasive Celtic

49

influence in our music; bodhrans and Celtic harps are among the hundreds of new and restored instruments that hang from the store's rafters.

Zwicker's Gallery (6) is just around the corner on Doyle Street. Look for works by established Nova Scotian artists including Alex Colville and Ken Tolmie. The gallery also has a large selection of antique prints and maps, along with 19th century engravings of Halifax.

At the end of Doyle, turn right onto Queen Street. The cluster of buildings on your right comprise **Royal Artillery Park (7)**. Two of these, the residence of the General Commanding Officer and the Officers' Mess, are "among the city's most valuable historic resources," according to Elizabeth

Pacey, a leading authority on Halifax architecture (Pacey's excellent books on the subject include *Georgian Halifax, Historic Halifax* and *Landmarks: Historic Buildings of Nova Scotia*). These unassuming wooden buildings, best viewed from the Sackville Street side of the park, are the sole survivors of the many wooden buildings that once housed army regiments in the early 1800s.

Still an active military complex, most of the park is off-limits to the public. However, the **Cambridge Military Library (8)**, a tidy, century-old brick building visible from Queen Street, is open weekdays. To be transported back to the world of a 19th century English gentleman, visit the library's magnificent reading room, with its high ceilings, leather chairs and plush carpet. You can almost smell the cigars and taste the brandy. The library's collection includes rare books that were shipped to Halifax from the Corfu Garrison Library

THE CAMBRIDGE MILITARY LIBRARY

when the British ended their occupation of the island in 1864.

At the corner of Queen and Birmingham streets is the studio of jeweller **James Bradshaw (9)**. An accomplished goldsmith, Bradshaw likes to work with "ideal cut" diamonds from Lazare, the same company that supplies Tiffany's. Bradshaw's uncompromising standards are revealed in his jewellery and in the studio driveway, where he parks his Porsche.

A few doors further along Birmingham Street is **Woozles (10)** (a slight detour from the suggested tour). This fine children's bookstore actively promotes local writers; knowledgeable staff can help you find the best Nova Scotian books for young readers.

Continue to the end of Queen Street (you are now facing the south slope of Citadel Hill). The private home to your left, **Bollard House (11)**, has been putting a hitch in the step of passersby for more than a century. A jog in Queen Street caused by the expansion of Royal Artillery Park early in the 19th century, and the later extension of Dresden Row to Sackville Street, left a vacant trapezoidal plot where the ingenious owner of the adjacent house eventually built the

quirky hip-roofed section that stands in front of you. Antique dealers and artists have long been interested in the home. Legend has it that one of the elderly sisters who lived here after the Second World War, fed up with the constant attention, chopped up a ship's figurehead in the attic — one less antique for the vultures who swarmed below!

Turn left onto Dresden Row and head back toward Spring Garden Road. If you, or someone you know, loves books about the sea, be sure to stop at **Nautica Booksellers (12)**. You will find Halifax's best selection of rare and used books on nautical themes: naval, mercantile, ocean sciences, technical, diving, whaling, piracy, polar, yachting, law, literature, and travel.

Scanway Restaurant (13) is a few doors down. You'll probably want to

sample Nova Scotia seafood while in Halifax, and you won't find any better than the light Scandinavian dishes prepared here. Enjoy an excellent Scanway dessert and coffee in the pastry shop. **Brothers Deli and Cafe (14)** is a good spot for a quick lunch. You may decide to bolster your resources at the **American Express Office (15)** on Dresden Row before reentering Spring Garden Road; no matter which way you turn, left or right, you will be tempted by some of the city's best shops.

You might want a refreshment first. The **Thirsty Duck (16)** pub, at the corner of Spring Garden and Queen, is often crowded and noisy in the evenings, but provides a relaxed atmosphere for an afternoon drink. If you are hungry as well, **Il Mercato (17)** is a recent and very successful addition to the Halifax scene. It features northern Italian style pastas, pizzas and grilled fish or meat at moderate prices. The place is usually jammed at meal times and busy the rest of the day.

Cross the street to **Mills Brothers (18)**, a fine, old-

fashioned department store that has been serving Haligonians since 1919. Imported gifts, along with men's and women's clothing, accessories and cosmetics, are tastefully displayed throughout Mills' spacious interior. For years, the store's imaginative Christmas windows have been a pleasant diversion for frantic shoppers.

Continue along Spring Garden Road to **Jennifer's of Nova Scotia (19)**. Trinket-sized souvenirs and prized works by Nova Scotia's best artisans are all part of Jennifer's eclectic inventory. Handknit woolens and wheel-thrown pottery are among the most popular gift items.

There are several upscale shopping centres in the area. **Queen's Court (20)**, **City Centre Atlantic (21)**, **Spring Garden Place (22)** and **Park Lane Mall (23)** are full of the specialty shops and services that once lined the street. Spring Garden Place serves up a variety of treats. On the market level, Pastamimi and the Rye'n Pickle Deli are popular luncheon spots. Or you may choose the fixings for a great picnic lunch at Spring Garden Grocery (perhaps, to be enjoyed later at Point Pleasant Park). Port of Wines offers a wide selection of imported

wines and spirits. Local favourites from Jost and Sainte-Famille, the province's two wineries, are also available. Upstairs, Ryan Duffy's is a traditional steak house where corn-fed striploin and Caesar salad are perennial favourites. Casual fare and a quiet drink are available in the adjoining pub.

Frog Hollow, also in Spring Garden Place, is a small

bookstore with surprisingly strong literature and women's sections. Across the street, **Entitlement (24)**, next to the Lord Nelson Hotel, is the largest bookstore in the Spring Garden Road area and perfectly suited for browsing. Its well-stocked shelves include a wide variety of regional books. You may also find what you're looking for at the **Bookmark (25)** or at Smith Books in the Park Lane Mall (there are also movie theatres here).

A few doors along from the Bookmark is the **Daily Grind (26)**, with a wide range of newspapers and magazines at the front and a pleasant café at the back.

Anchoring this end of Spring Garden Road is the **Lord**

Nelson Hotel (27). Its great location attracts a loyal clientele, and the lobby is a fine public space.

Just up the street adjoining the CBC Radio building is a parking lot which, until 1993, was the site of the boyhood home of novelist Hugh MacLennan **(28)**. Local heritage groups and book publishers came up with a proposal to save this last of what

THE MACLENNAN
FAMILY HOUSE,
DEMOLISHED BY THE
CBC

PUBLIC GARDENS GATES WERE SHIPPED FROM SCOTLAND IN 1890

BELOW: GRIFFIN'S POND

was once a row of Victorian family homes overlooking the Public Gardens. Incredibly, local CBC managers insisted on demolishing the house and neither CBC senior managers nor the board were prepared to stop them.

Having passed through the shopping district, there is no better place to restore the soul than the **Public Gardens (29)**. A cherished Halifax landmark since the 1830s, these formal Victorian gardens are the oldest, and many say the finest, in North America. Do not pass them by!

The gardens were started by a group of prominent Haligonians who wanted a place to indulge their passion for the "cultivation of choice fruit trees, vegetables, rare plants and flowers." Naturally, the Nova Scotia Horticultural Society, as they called themselves, chose a site along fashionable Spring Garden

Road. The garden quickly became an aesthetic success and a financial burden — with only slight relief coming from the cultivation and sale of rhubarb by the Society. Government assistance came, but with strings attached; the Society was to make its garden public on a part-time basis.

The city eventually took over the garden in 1874 and combined it with an adjoining civic garden which had been started a few years earlier. Superintendent Richard Power, who had gardened for the Duke of Devonshire in Ireland, devised a plan that remains remarkably intact (Power family members cared for the Gardens until the 1960s).

Power did a magnificent job. Pathways, shaded by beautiful weeping trees,

meander past floating beds of spring daffodils or summer fuchsia. Subtropical plantings and unusual trees from around the world lend an exotic atmosphere that typified formal Victorian gardens. Griffin's Pond recalls the days when the Freshwater River flowed through the town, making its way to Pleasant Street (now the south end of Barrington Street) and the "Kissing Bridge", before spilling into the harbour. The river and the bridge are gone, but the Gardens are still in full bloom.

At the centre of it all stands the gazebo built to commemorate the Golden Jubilee of Queen Victoria in 1887. Concerts are held here on summer Sunday afternoons. On Saturdays, brides, grooms and attendants can be seen posing for photographers.

Information on the Public Gardens and other city attractions is available from the **Visitor Information Centre (30)** located at the corner of South Park and Sackville streets, just outside the northeast entrance to the Gardens.

SOUTH END AND
POINT PLEASANT PARK

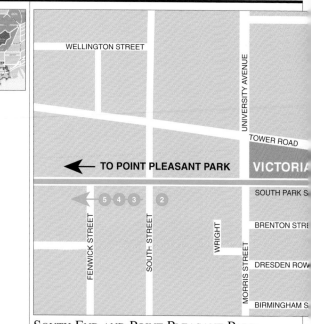

WELLINGTON STREET

UNIVERSITY AVENUE

TOWER ROAD

← TO POINT PLEASANT PARK VICTORI

SOUTH PARK S

5 4 3 2

BRENTON STRE

FENWICK STREET

SOUTH STREET

WRIGHT

MORRIS STREET

DRESDEN ROW

BIRMINGHAM S

SOUTH END AND POINT PLEASANT PARK

If your spirit needs unbending, then take a long afternoon — preferably a sunny one — for this leisurely stroll to Point Pleasant Park. A great spot for a picnic lunch, you can fill your basket with food and drink from the market at Spring Garden Place (near the corner of Spring Garden Road and South Park Street, where this tour begins).

Point Pleasant has been an oasis for Haligonians since Lieutenant-Governor Fanning built his estate here, complete with showy gardens, late in the 18th century. Spectacular views of the Harbour Approaches and the Northwest Arm that attracted sightseers, also caught the eye of the military establishment. As you amble along the park's shady walkways, you will pass by several old fortifications, including the Prince of Wales Tower, now a National Historic Site.

On your way to Point Pleasant, keep a look out for many of the city's finest homes. Grand Victorian mansions line South Park Street and Young Avenue. Like the commercial buildings of Barrington Street, they were built during an unprecedented boom at the turn of the century. Circular driveways recall the days when fashionable Haligonians made social rounds by horse and carriage. Although several of these houses have been divided into flats, Young Avenue remains a prestige address.

Begin your tour at **Victoria Park (1)**, across the street from the Public Gardens, at the corner of Spring Garden

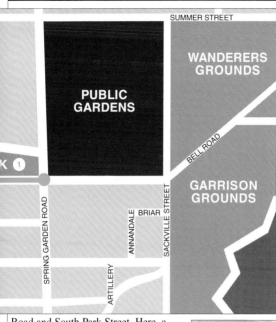

SUMMER STREET

WANDERERS GROUNDS

PUBLIC GARDENS

BELL ROAD

GARRISON GROUNDS

SPRING GARDEN ROAD

ANNANDALE

BRIAR

SACKVILLE STREET

ARTILLERY

BELOW: VIEW OF HALIFAX FROM FORT NEEDHAM

Road and South Park Street. Here, a statue of beloved poet Robert Burns signifies the sentimental attachment of "New Scotland" to Old. Further on, you may spot summer students from nearby Dalhousie University sunning themselves near the park's fountain. There is often a chip wagon stationed along here, dispensing the delicious alternative to a healthy lunch.

It does not take long for the lavish houses to appear. The three homes at the southwest corner of South Park and Morris streets were built in the Queen Anne Revival style, a popular choice of wealthy Haligonians toward the end of the 19th century. Look for the triangular pediments atop the arched Palladian windows that characterize Queen Anne houses. The style reached its zenith in the turreted palaces that you will see further along on Young Avenue.

Turn left on South Street to see the **Heart of Sorrows Chapel (2)** in Holy Cross Cemetery. On August 31, 1843 nearly 2000 people congregated at this site to build the chapel in a single day. Inside, the French stained glass windows date from the 16th and 17th centuries. Heart of Sorrows is open year round, Monday to Friday, 8:30am to 4:30pm.

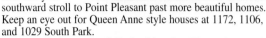

Back on South Park Street, continue your southward stroll to Point Pleasant past more beautiful homes. Keep an eye out for Queen Anne style houses at 1172, 1106, and 1029 South Park.

At Inglis Street, South Park widens into Young Avenue. A quick jog left on Inglis takes you to historic **Thorndean House (3)**, at number 5680. Built in 1834, this handsome

Georgian home in the Classic Revival style has a colourful past. In 1838, Thorndean was bought by James Forman, one of several prominent Halifax businessmen who had successfully petitioned the House of Assembly for the incorporation of the Bank of Nova Scotia in 1832. Forman became chief cashier (general manager) of the new bank. An esteemed Haligonian, he suddenly fell from grace in 1870, when a junior clerk discovered that Forman had defrauded the bank of more than $300,000 during his lengthy term as cashier. With his career and health in ruins, Forman slunk off to London, where he died a short time later. It seems his ghost lingered for a while; a furtive, top-hatted figure has been seen emanating from an old well in the kitchen basement of Thorndean. The well has since been filled in!

Retrace your steps to the corner of Inglis and Young Avenue. There is yet another lavish Queen Anne style residence at **989 Young (4)**. It was built in 1903 for Halifax businessman George Wright (for more on Wright and his untimely

death in 1912 see p. 28). The house, like several others on Young Avenue, was designed by Cape Breton-born architect James C. Dumaresq. Generally considered the best Nova Scotian architect of his day, Dumaresq also designed many of the commercial buildings on the west side of

Barrington Street, including the Wright Building in 1896.

You will be flanked by elegant mansions as you continue along Young Avenue. Pause at the bridge that crosses over the **CN Rail (5)** main line. You are at the end of an ambitious railway cutting that runs the length of the Halifax Peninsula. Some of the rock blasted from here was used as fill for the Ports Canada deepwater piers to your left. The huge grain elevators, part of the port complex, store Prairie grain prior to shipment overseas. Cruise ships dock at the piers during the late summer and fall.

Pass through the open iron gates at the end of Young Avenue and turn right onto Point Pleasant Drive. The beautiful stone lodge that you see, another Dumaresq design, was built in 1896 as the official residence for the Keeper of Point Pleasant Park. Just ahead, to the left, is the park's western entrance.

Point Pleasant (6) could very easily have become the location of downtown Halifax instead of the city's favourite park. In 1749, Governor Cornwallis wanted to build the new

TOP: FORMER HOME OF GEORGE WRIGHT, 989 YOUNG AVENUE

MIDDLE: RAILWAY-YARD SEEN FROM YOUNG AVENUE

BOTTOM: HALTERM CONTAINER FACILITY FROM THE WATER

LEFT: PARK GATE AT THE END OF YOUNG AVENUE

Chain Rock
Battery

8

PARKING 6

TOWER ROAD

ARM ROAD

MAPLE ROAD

SERPENTINE ROAD

CABLE ROAD

TOWER HILL ROAD

7

CAMBRIDGE DRIVE

YOUNG AVENUE

Martello
Tower

CEDAR WALK

BIRCH ROAD

OGILVIE RD.

FIR WALK

HEATHER ROAD

MAPLE WALK

BRIDAL PATHS

PINE ROAD

9

Commonwealth
Wars Memorial

PRINCE OF WALES DRIVE

FORT ROAD

POINT PLEASANT DRIVE

10

Point Pleasant
Battery

SHORE ROAD

13

Black Rock
Beach

11

Shannon and
Chesapeake
Memorial

12

Sailors'
Peacetime
Memorial

PARKING

BREAKWATER

NATIONAL HARBOURS BOARD
CONTAINER PIER

14

BELOW: YOUNG
AVENUE FROM THE
PARK

garrison town here, as it was a site easily defended from land attacks. But sailors were wary of nasty, onshore southeasterlies and the rocky shoals that ringed the Point. So Halifax was built on the harbour slope of Citadel Hill, while Point Pleasant became an important part of the town's defence complex. The forest was left standing to hide

fortifications from enemy eyes. By the mid-19th century, Point Pleasant was valued more as a place where people took their ease than as a strategic location (although its military function was by no means exhausted). In 1866, on the eve of Confederation, the British Government agreed to lease the 186 acres of wooded parkland to Halifax for 999 years at the nominal sum of one shilling per year (about ten cents). The shilling ceremony takes place each summer at the park.

Use the map in the parking lot near the western entrance (at Tower Road and Point Pleasant Drive) to plan your walk around Point Pleasant, or simply wander along the meandering pathways. The description that follows will take you around the park in a counter-

clockwise direction, bypassing the ruins of some of the old fortifications that you may decide to visit on your own.

The **Prince of Wales Martello Tower (7)** is nearby. It was commissioned by Prince Edward (Queen Victoria's father) in 1796, during his six-year tenure as commander of the Halifax garrison. Like others, Edward had been impressed by accounts of a round defence tower on Cape Mortella, in Corsica, that had withstood a pounding by two British warships in 1794. These "Martello" towers became all the rage. The Prince of Wales Tower, named for Edward's favourite brother, introduced the trendy fortification to North America. In Halifax, other Martello towers soon followed — one, further out the harbour at York Redoubt, and, another, at Fort Clarence (now the site of the Mauger's Beach Lighthouse, on McNab's Island).

LEFT: MAUGER'S BEACH LIGHTHOUSE

Today, the Prince of Wales Tower is open to visitors during the summer months. Exhibits explain the history of the tower and its strategic importance; Parks Canada staff are on hand to answer questions.

The **Chain Rock Battery (8)**, overlooking the Northwest Arm, was another important link in the town's seaward defences. From here, a chain boom once stretched across the water to defend against enemy warships. Today, the Northwest Arm is a haven for pleasure craft. There are two yacht clubs on the opposite shore. On fair summer days, this is a good place to watch the bright splash of spinnakers against the blue waters of the Arm, the perfect backdrop for a picnic.

COMMONWEALTH WARS MEMORIAL

Toward the end of the Point, not far from the shore, is a patch of wild heather, a rarity outside Scotland. Legend has it that soldiers from a Scottish regiment shook their heather-filled mattresses over this spot while stationed here long ago. Some seeds fell out and took root.

Close by, the **Commonwealth Wars Memorial (9)** remembers those who lost their lives at sea. Further along, the **Point Pleasant Battery (10)** (established in 1762), together with the Ives Battery on McNab's Island, guarded the entrance to Halifax Harbour for nearly two centuries. During the First World War, mines were laid between Point Pleasant and McNab's, leaving a narrow channel lit by searchlights. Later, a steel anti-submarine net was added. Both batteries stood at the ready for the attack that never came.

It's easy to see why the Point Pleasant Battery remained so important for so long. There is a commanding view from here. Cast your eyes seaward and you will probably spot some sort of ocean-going vessel; navy frigates, container ships, general cargo ships, and cruise ships all ply these waters.

Walk round the point, past the **Shannon and Chesapeake Memorial (11)** (for more on the *Chesapeake's* capture see p. 33), and the **huge anchor (12)** commemorating sailors lost in peacetime, to **Black Rock Beach (13)**. Sunbathers still gather here although swimming is now discouraged (there are plans afoot to clean up the harbour). You may see cormorants (known locally as shags) drying their wings as they perch on the rocks that give the beach its name. The Halifax City police officer who frequently patrols this area on horseback is an especial favourite of children.

Close by, is the **Halterm (14)** container facility, a reminder of the busy world that this tour left behind. Hopefully, you are now sufficiently restored to exit the park via Point Pleasant Drive and ease your way back into the 20th century.

5

FERRY TRIP TO DARTMOUTH

MAPLEHURST DRIVE

HAZELHURST STREET

PARKER

NEWCASTLE STREET

PLEASANT STREET

OLD FERRY ROAD

LEA

LINDEN

ST. GEORGES LANE

BLINK BON NIE

MAITLAND STH

CAN

ALBERT STREET

PORT

HAWTHOR

FERRY TRIP TO DARTMOUTH

This tour takes you across the harbour to Dartmouth by passenger ferry. Dartmouth was founded a year after Halifax, when 353 settlers arrived from southwestern England aboard the *Alderney* in 1750. Long before that, the site was occupied seasonally by the Mi'kmaq who canoed and portaged across the mainland each spring after wintering along the shores of the Bay of Fundy (later, builders of the Shubenacadie Canal would follow their

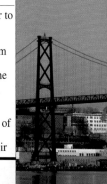

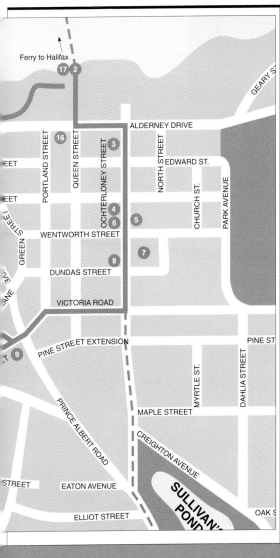

Ferry to Halifax

GEARY ST

ALDERNEY DRIVE

PORTLAND STREET

QUEEN STREET

OCHTERLONEY STREET

NORTH STREET

EDWARD ST.

CHURCH ST.

PARK AVENUE

EET

EET

GREEN STREET

WENTWORTH STREET

DUNDAS STREET

VICTORIA ROAD

PINE STREET EXTENSION

PINE ST

MYRTLE ST.

DAHLIA STREET

PRINCE ALBERT ROAD

MAPLE STREET

CREIGHTON AVENUE

SULLIVAN'S POND

EATON AVENUE

STREET

ELLIOT STREET

OAK S

ANGUS L. MACDONALD BRIDGE

route exactly). The Mi'kmaq resisted the colonization of their lands by the British, launching raids against the new settlers on both sides of the harbour. Life in Dartmouth was especially perilous until a 1752 treaty with the Mi'kmaq brought peace.

From the beginning, Halifax and Dartmouth have been joined at the harbour. John Connor began operating a ferry service in 1752, charging three cents for the hour long rowboat trip to the opposite shore. The ferry — powered in turn by wind, steam, and diesel fuel — has been running ever since. This century, ties between the sister cities were further strengthened with the construction of two bridges, the Angus L. Macdonald (completed in 1955) and the A. Murray MacKay (1970). They channel the ebb and flow of commuter

traffic across the harbour. While the bridges also afford some spectacular views, it is the ferry that puts you face to face with the salt water and wind and brings the harbour to life. And, at one dollar per crossing, it remains a great bargain.

Begin your tour at the **Halifax Ferry Terminal (1)**, where you will probably want to buy two tokens to get you across to Dartmouth and back again. The ferry leaves every 15 minutes at peak times during weekdays, and half hourly at other times including Saturdays (Sunday service is available from June to September, noon to 6pm). There is a lot to see during the ten minute crossing. Look out

RIGHT: CANADIAN COAST GUARD VESSELS

the harbour to George's Island, with its old fortification and lighthouse. Harbour traffic is monitored from the golfball-like radio antenna in the middle of the island. In the opposite direction, the two bridges — the Macdonald in the foreground and the MacKay further on — span the Narrows that open into the Bedford Basin. The naval dockyard lies near the foot of the Macdonald Bridge on the Halifax side. Here, you will often see frigates, destroyer escorts, and operational support ships — the large, black numbers on their battle-grey hulls holding the key to otherwise secret identities.

Further along toward the MacKay bridge is the site of the Halifax Explosion. Here, on a clear December morning in 1917, the French munitions ship *Mont Blanc* collided with the Belgian relief ship *Imo*, leveling the north ends of both cities and killing nearly 2,000 people.

Ahead, you will see the distinctive red and white hulled vessels of the Canadian Coast Guard. The modern building to the left is the **Dartmouth Ferry Terminal (2)**. You just have time for few lungfuls of salt sea air before disembarking.

GRACE UNITED CHURCH

Walk up the steps from the terminal building to Alderney Drive. Turn left, continue for a short distance, then turn right onto Ochterloney Street. **Tea and Temptations (3)** serves delicious afternoon teas from the historic premises at number 44. The house was built for William Coleman, a 19th century captain of the Dartmouth ferry. The five-sided dormers in the gable roof were a popular innovation that came across the Atlantic with the Scottish stonemasons who built the Shubenacadie Canal (see p. 73).

Further up Ochterloney, you will pass by **Grace United Church (4)**, one of many buildings in the area to rise from the ashes of the Halifax Explosion. Thankfully, all was not lost in the devastation. One notable survivor was the **Quaker House (5)** at 57-59 Ochterloney. Built in 1786, this is

Dartmouth's oldest extant house and a relic from one of the most interesting chapters of the city's history.

Following the American Revolution, Britain slapped high tariffs on goods from the United States. Among those who suffered, was a group of Quaker whalers from Nantucket who had been supplying the English with sperm oil for street lamps, medicines, and cosmetics (they also met the

considerable demand for whale bone corsets). In 1785, 24 families moved their whaling enterprise to Dartmouth, attracted by a Nova Scotia government subsidy on housing and a colony that was still very British. Their industry flourished along the Dartmouth waterfront until 1791, when the British government pressured them to relocate to Milford Haven, in Wales.

William Ray, a cooper, lived in the salt box house at 59 Ochterloney (the roof was later lifted and bedrooms added to the second floor). Ray held the esteemed position of Inspector

of Oil at Dartmouth. Today, his house has been partially restored by the Dartmouth Museum Society. Guides in period costume tell the Quaker Whalers' story. The house is open June 1 to Sept. 1, from 9am to 5pm.

Just up the street, on the opposite side, is the **Masonic Hall (6)**, built for the Eastern Star Lodge in 1909. Its classical two-storey pilasters and impressive keystone arch atop the central window befit the Freemasons' devotion to the ideals of construction.

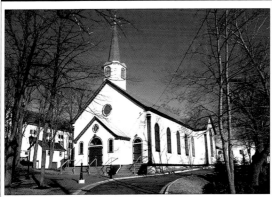

LEFT: CHRIST
CHURCH

BELOW: FIRST
BAPTIST CHURCH

Across the street, **Christ Church (7)**, built in 1817, is Dartmouth's oldest church. Its wooden walls withstood the blast of the Halifax Explosion. Unfortunately, Christ Church is not open to the public. Further along, the rubble stone **First Baptist Church (8)** was built in 1922 to replace yet another casualty of the Explosion. Its peculiar style reflects the popularity of the British Arts and Crafts movement of the time.

Walk along Ochterloney Street to Victoria Road. If you have the time and a sunny day, then you may decide to continue straight on to feed the ducks at Sullivan's Pond or take your ease on the shores of Lake Banook. Banook has played host to national and international regattas; during the summer, you will often see international calibre rowers and canoeists straining at their oars and paddles. The lake is also the site of Dartmouth's Natal Day celebrations, held each year on the first weekend of August.

OCHTERLONEY
STREET MURALS

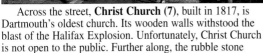

To follow the tour, turn right onto Victoria Road, continue along to the traffic light, then cross Prince Albert Road to Portland Street. As you walk by **St. James United Church (9)**, look carefully at the granite blocks that make up the retaining wall alongside the sidewalk. Several of these were salvaged from the abandoned locks of the Shubenacadie Canal and bear the trademarks of the Scottish stonemasons who carved them (a fitting reminder of St. James' Presbyterian roots).

Walk up Portland Street to "Five Corners", then turn right onto Albert Street. At **no. 3 Albert (10)**, Tom Forrestall displays his new

BELOW:
THE *POINT VIGOUR*

A. Macdonald. The *Macdonald* escorted the *SS Manhattan* on her historic 1969 crossing through the Northwest Passage; the propeller was sheared off by ice.

Before returning to Halifax, you may decide to dine at one of the two excellent restaurants that are close at hand. **La Perla (16)**, at the top of the steps leading up from the terminal to Alderney Drive, features northern Italian cuisine in intimate surroundings. **MacAskill's (17)**, in the terminal building, offers a varied menu with seafood specialties and a

sweeping view of the harbour and the Halifax shoreline.

If you time things right and the weather cooperates, then your ferry trip back to Halifax will be a sunset cruise.

6

EXCURSIONS

EXCURSIONS

Depending on the length of your visit, you may decide to take a day trip outside the city. There are several rewarding destinations — all within about an hour's drive of Halifax.

At Peggy's Cove, southwest of Halifax, and all along the coastline to the east of the city, you will find the rugged

seascapes most often associated with Nova Scotia. But you will also find near-perfect harbours along the South Shore at towns like Chester, Mahone Bay, and Lunenburg. Here, privateers and rum-runners once unshipped dangerous cargoes; now, pleasure seekers moor their yachts. These are among the most storied and picturesque towns in the province — each deserving of an unhurried visit. Or you may simply want to spend a day at the beach. There are broad sweeps of fine, white sand all along Nova Scotia's Atlantic shore. The water can be invigorating to say the least (much more Labrador Current than Gulf Stream!), but there is no better tonic for the weary traveller than a stroll along the Atlantic strand.

If possible, save your excursions for fair weather. All of these destinations are flattered by sunshine, and there is plenty to do in the city on a rainy day.

PEGGY'S COVE

Peggy's Cove is a 30-40 minute drive from Halifax along Route 333. The Cove, with its vivid, pitched-roof houses perched atop a mass of granite overlooking the snug harbour, has been exposed on miles of film and acres of canvas. It has become the postcard profile of an east coast fishing village.

Peggy's Cove was not always held in such high esteem. Before the economic hard times of the 1920s and '30s, villages like Peggy's Cove were seen as backward, not quaint. But the failure of industry in Nova Scotia prompted the assertion that fishing villages and rugged seascapes had always been more real — more Nova Scotian — than the illusory progress of the late 19th and early 20th centuries. Peggy's Cove was now the very essence of Nova Scotia, a desolate boundary where land meets sea.

LIGHTHOUSE AT PEGGY'S COVE

The successful promotion of Peggy's Cove has led to a curious irony. You are exhorted to discover the unspoiled beauty of Peggy's Cove in the company of tens or even hundreds of other people (the Cove is a mandatory stop for most North American coach tours to Nova Scotia). There is a busy restaurant and gift shop and the old lighthouse now serves as a post office.

But something truly elemental is still revealed at Peggy's Cove — something about the human spirit in the face of adversity. If you visit on a day when a stiff onshore breeze sends waves crashing against the rocks (heed the warnings to keep your distance), you will marvel at the pluck of those who chose to live here. You can see something of that spirit in sculptor William deGarthe's "lasting monument to Canadian fishermen", hewn into the granite outcrop behind his house. The sculpture's guardian angel is a reminder: Peggy's Cove is more than just quaint.

CHESTER

The village of Chester lies across three fingers of a peninsula that overlooks Mahone Bay. With its 365-odd islands ("one for each day of the year"), the bay is a sailor's paradise. The village itself is a New England resort town that just happened to end up in Nova Scotia. Appropriately, Chester's first settlers (it was called Shoreham then) sailed from Boston in 1759; much of the rest of Mahone Bay was colonized by Germans, French, and Swiss. Although Chester is also increasingly the haunt of yachting enthusiasts from Halifax and Toronto, its predominantly Cape Cod-style architecture and the Yankee accents of many of its summer residents still give the town an unmistakable New England flavour.

The Parade Grounds off South Street, site of the Yacht Club, a band stand, a war memorial, and a salt-water swimming pool (the Lido), provide the best vantage point for viewing the sleek yachts in Chester's Front and Back Harbours. Take a trip along "The Peninsula", at the western boundary of Front Harbour, to see the grand houses that are among Chester's main attractions.

If you are looking to spend a special evening outside Halifax, then Chester is a good bet. Dine at The Galley in nearby Marriott's

Cove or at the Captain's House on Central Street. Both feature delicious seafood and unforgettable views of the water. Then, take in a show at the Chester Playhouse,

which offers live theatre throughout the summer months.

Even a brief visit to Chester makes it easy to see why so many who could choose to spend their summers anywhere, choose to spend them here.

MAHONE BAY

Be sure to take the old road (Route 3) to get to Mahone Bay. The road dips and winds its way along the shore until a long, sweeping bend brings one of Nova Scotia's most recognizable landscapes into view. Colourful buildings and wharves, monuments to Mahone Bay's seafaring past, line

RIGHT: THREE CHURCHES AT MAHONE BAY

the waterfront of the town's pretty harbour. Sailboats and other pleasure craft are moored offshore. And three fine 19th-century churches — United, Lutheran, and Anglican — stand "side by each" at the head of the harbour.

Once a flourishing shipbuilding centre, Mahone Bay is now known for its crafts and antiques. Fine shops — the kind that have given way to malls in so many other places — occupy buildings formerly used in the shipping trade. Expect high standards and innovative designs at the pottery, pewter, and rug-hooking studios that line Main Street. You should have no trouble finding a lasting memento of your Nova Scotia vacation.

ST. JOHN'S ANGLICAN CHURCH, LUNENBURG

LUNENBURG

Find time for Lunenburg during your visit to Nova Scotia. Its German heritage, rich seafaring tradition, and outstanding architecture make Lunenburg a truly special place. "Old Town", built in 1753 on the slope rising up from the north shore of the harbour, was recently designated a National Historic District by the Government of Canada.

Lunenburg represents the second attempt made by British

authorities to colonize Nova Scotia (Halifax was their first). Britain seemed the obvious source of colonists, but the labour of prospective emigrants was a valuable commodity back home. The government also feared the destabilization that might result from a significant emigration of Protestants. So they recruited "Foreign Protestants" from parts of what are now Germany, Switzerland, and France. Many of these settled at Lunenburg in 1753.

Today, those looking for signs of German ethnicity in the town will find them in the Lutheran Church, which is still vital, and in traces of the "Lunenburg Dutch" dialect (the *th* sound is often pronounced *t* or *d*). Local restaurants serve potato soup, Lunenburg pudding, and sauerkraut — all dishes with German origins — alongside some of Nova Scotia's best seafood cuisine.

"LUNENBURG BUMP"

Though farmers by nature, it was not long before Lunenburgers turned to the sea for their livelihoods. The town's offshore fishing fleet won international recognition (in the 19th century, cod that was dried and salted to produce the "Lunenburg Cure" was in great demand in the West Indies). So did Lunenburg boatbuilders. Their lofty reputation was assured with the 1921 construction of the 285-ton racing schooner *Bluenose*, never defeated in Nova Scotian waters.

The town's seafaring heritage is celebrated at the outstanding Fisheries Museum of the Atlantic on Montague Street. At the opposite end of Montague, the business of building and repairing boats is still carried on. Here, you will find the last working dory shop in the province and the Scotia Trawlers shipyard (formerly the Smith and Rhuland boatyards, where both the *Bluenose* and *Bluenose II* were built).

ABOVE: LUNENBURG IS A CENTRE FOR CRAFTS

BELOW: DORY BUILDING

Then there are the houses. Lunenburg's distinctive architecture is unrivalled in Nova Scotia. A number of 18th-century dwellings survive, one-storey Cape Cod style houses or two-storey homes in the British Classical tradition. Look for them along the harbour slope above the Fisheries Museum, on York, Prince, Pelham, and Townsend Streets.

Nineteenth-century buildings dominate Old Town. Scottish dormer windows were added to many of these British Classical homes. Later, the dormers were moved down the slopes of roofs to hang over central doorways. You will see this "Lunenburg Bump" throughout Old Town. It can be quite ostentatious and was probably a reflection of the town's success in the salt fish trade.

Fewer than a third of the houses in Old Town were built after 1900. Even these — many of them wooden and restrained by relatively small lots — do not seriously compromise Lunenburg's architectural integrity.

There are several great festivals held in Lunenburg throughout the summer months. Ask at any Visitor Information Centre for schedules and other details concerning Lunenburg's Craft Festival (July), Folk Harbour Festival (August), and Fisheries Exhibition (August). You may be able to plan your excursion around one of them.

79

SALTWATER BEACHES

On a hot day when you have no particular plans, you may decide to simply beach it. There are several fine, saltwater beaches within easy driving distance of Halifax and Dartmouth. Before leaving, pay attention to the wind direction. If the breeze is onshore, then it can be several degrees cooler along the coast than it is in the city. Take along a sweater just in case.

Crystal Crescent Beach is 29 km (18 mi.) south of Halifax along Route 349. Here, you will find an unsupervised stretch of fine, grey sand. The beach is relatively exposed, making for invigorating water temperatures and some good-sized waves in an onshore wind.

Queensland, on Route 3 just before Hubbards, is one of the most popular beaches on the South Shore. It is supervised during July and August. It is not a large beach, so come here when you are feeling sociable.

Rainbow Haven, 8 km (5 mi.) east of Cow Bay on the outskirts of Dartmouth, is another local favourite. This large, unsupervised sand and cobble beach at the entrance to Cole Harbour is more sheltered and usually warmer than other beaches along this shore. Rainbow Haven has change and canteen facilities.

Lawrencetown Beach is just east of Dartmouth on Route 207, at Lawrencetown. This steep, sandy beach is supervised and has change and canteen facilities. Exposed to the Atlantic, Lawrencetown's large waves make it a favourite with Nova Scotia surfers.

Martinique Beach (supervised), 11 km (7 mi.) south of Musquodoboit Harbour on the East Petpeswick Road, is a little further from the city. As a result, on some summer days you will have this five-kilometre (3 mi.) long stretch to yourself. The fine sand hardens at the waterline, making Martinique ideal for long walks. As for swimming, the temperature of the crystal-clear water belies the beach's tropical name. After a dip here, you will return to the city refreshed in the extreme.

DINING, ACCOMMODATIONS, ATTRACTIONS, AND ACTIVITIES

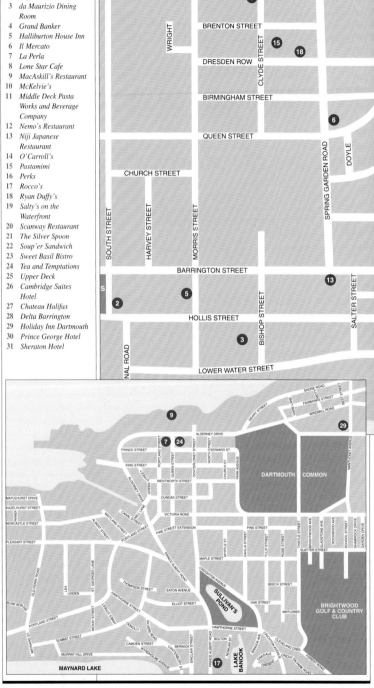

DINING

This list of recommended Halifax restaurants has been compiled with the help of Elaine Elliot and Virginia Lee, authors of the popular guidebook/cookbook *Maritime Flavours*. Our particular favourites are indicated with a star (★). The price ranges shown are inexpensive ($), moderate ($$), and expensive ($$$). Reservations are recommended for all these restaurants.

Le Bistro Cafe   1
*1333 South Park Street, Halifax, NS **423-8428***
$$ Major cards, wheelchair accessible, non-smoking area, open daily 11:30am - midnight
Le Bistro is a popular spot, and a good place for a snack or light meal on the off hours when more ambitious restaurants are closed. The style is (old-fashioned) Paris cafe with omelettes, crepes, and pasta. There's a bright patio-style area at the front, and even a few outdoor tables for warm sunny days.

Cafe Chianti 2
5163 South Street, Halifax, NS 423-7471
$$ Major cards, wheelchair accessible, non-smoking area, open daily for dinner
Cafe Chianti is an old-fashioned European cafe in style, with Chianti bottles hanging from the ceiling. The rooms are cosy and busily noisy; the food is good if somewhat old-fashioned and the weekend entertainment is first-rate. Here you will find northern Italian/eastern European specialities such as Linguini Marco Polo, Chicken Paprikash and a variety of dishes that accent their home-made sausage.

Chickenburger
1531 Bedford Highway, Bedford, NS 835-5194
$ No cards, non-smoking available, open 9:00 am - 1:00 am daily
Nova Scotians will say the Innes family serve the best chickenburgers in the country and they have been doing so for 50 odd years! The menu also includes wonderful hamburgers, fish and chips, and milkshakes. Have fun at this clean, fast, authentically 1950s diner.

★ da Maurizio Dining Room 3
1496 Lower Water Street, Halifax, NS 423-0859
$$-$$$ Major cards, accessibility to Wine Bar only, non-smoking area, Mon. - Sat., 5:00 pm - 10:00 pm
Occupying the lower level of a restored brewery, da Maurizio's offer continental cuisine in a setting of crisp linens and fine china. Appetizer specialities may include Nova Scotia smoked salmon, Atlantic mussels steamed with garlic, herbs and tomatoes, or an assortment of soups and salads. The extensive dinner menu features a variety of veal, poultry, beef, and seafood dishes, and several Italian-type desserts will complement your meal.

Grand Banker 4
1919 Upper Water Street, Halifax, NS 428-7852
$$$ Major cards, wheelchair accessible, non-smoking area, open 7 days a week for breakfast, lunch and dinner
Ever since the Halifax Sheraton opened its doors the Grand Banker has been known for its consistent fine dining in an elegant yet relaxed atmosphere. Serving breakfast, lunch, and dinner, the restaurant has gained a reputation for serving the best Sunday Brunch in Halifax.

Halliburton House Inn 5
5184 Morris Street, Halifax, NS 420-0658
$$$ Major cards, not wheelchair accessible, non-smoking area, open daily for lunch and dinner
House guests, as well as the general public, may enjoy the innovative menu offered at this historic inn. The dining room offers traditional fare, as well as a variety of original dishes featuring wild game. You might like to try Wild Boar Paté, Buffalo Steak served with Prairie Hunter Sauce, or Pheasant Sausage, but be sure to end your meal with one of their delectable desserts. A secluded patio offers seasonal out of doors dining options.

★ Il Mercato 6
Spring Garden Road, Halifax, NS **422-2866**
$ Major cards, wheelchair accessible, non-smoking area
Il Mercato in the middle of the bustling Spring Garden Road area is the liveliest and most enjoyable of Halifax's mid-priced restaurants. A limited menu features very fresh seafood, grilled meats, and imaginative pastas. The inviting antipasta trays, and homemade Italian ice creams have made this small cafe popular with both the lunch and dinner crowd. Expect a short wait at popular dining times — it's worth it.

The Italian Market
McCully Street, Halifax, NS **455-6124**
$
Set up for Italian expatriates and others who love the fare, the Italian Market sells groceries imported from the green, red, and white country. Their small deli will prepare a variety of authentic Italian sandwiches to eat in or take out as well as daily salads and pasta choices.

King Wah
6430 Quinpool Road, Halifax, NS **423-2587**
$ Wheelchair accessible, open 7 days a week, eat in or take out
The Szechuan and Cantonese fare is authentic and very good. Loyal Haligonians have been eating here for years.

La Perla 7
71 Alderney Drive, Dartmouth, NS **469-3241**
$$-$$$ Major cards, wheelchair accessible, non-smoking area, Mon.-Fri. 11:00 am-11:00 pm, Sat. & Sun. 5:00 pm - 11:00 pm
Located only a minute's walk from the Dartmouth ferry terminal, La Perla is an intimate restaurant noted for its northern Italian cuisine. You might like to try Zuppa Di Pesce Al Modenese, a delightful seafood chowder, or Vitello Al Contidina, veal scallopini with artichokes and asparagus in a Marsala wine cream sauce. A window table will ensure a view of the harbour and waterfront.

Lone Star Cafe 8
1599 Grafton St., Halifax, NS **422-8524**
$ Major cards, not wheelchair accessible, open daily for lunch and dinner
Tex-Mex fare in Nova Scotia interpretation — at Halifax's Lone Star Cafe you can watch your tortilla pass through the baking machine while you enjoy the country and western music. An ideal place to bring the family, the Lone Star's ample servings offer good value for your dollar in a fun-filled atmosphere.

MacAskill's Restaurant 9
88 Alderney Drive, Dartmouth, NS **466-3100**
$$-$$$ Major cards, wheelchair accessible, non-smoking area, lunch and dinner served daily, Mon. - Fri., dinner only Sat. and Sun.
Located upstairs in the Dartmouth ferry terminal, MacAskill's patrons are treated to a panoramic view of harbour activities and the Halifax shoreline. Patrons can expect a varied menu of traditional dishes including freshly baked breads, Nova Scotian seafoods, steaks, and sumptuous desserts.

McKelvie's 10
1680 Lower Water Street, Halifax, NS 421-6161
$$ Major cards, wheelchair accessible, non-smoking area,
11:30am - 10:00 pm daily
Located in a turn-of-the-century fire station, this casual
restaurant boasts that "if it comes from the ocean it will
likely be on the menu." With a quick glance you will see that
this is true; however, they neglect to mention their steak,
pasta, and chicken offerings, many served Cajun-style.

Middle Deck Pasta Works and Beverage Company 11
Privateers' Warehouse, Historic Properties, Halifax, NS 425-1500
$-$$ Major cards, not wheelchair accessible, non-smoking
area, open daily for lunch and dinner
"Pasta Works", part of the Privateers' Wharf complex in
Historic Properties offers casual dining in a relaxed
atmosphere. The servings are ample and the extensive menu
features seafood, an assortment of pasta dishes, plus an
extensive dessert list.

Nemo's Restaurant 12
1865 Hollis Street, Halifax, NS 425-6738
$$ Major cards, wheelchair accessible, non-smoking area,
Mon. - Sat. for lunch and dinner, Sunday dinner only
Tucked in a 19th century stone building, Nemo's is a short
stroll from major downtown hotels. While the chef gives
special attention to several seafood selections, the menu
includes offerings from various cuisines, including
Provençale and northern Italian.

Niji Japanese Restaurant 13
1505 Barrington Street, Halifax, NS 422-1576
$$ Major cards, limited accessibility,
At Niji, Halifax's only Japanese restaurant you can watch the
chef with his flying knives prepare your dinner at the teppan
table or dine in the more intimate Japanese dining room.
Popular for its extensive Sushi bar, Niji provides authentic
cuisine in an Oriental setting.

O'Carroll's 14
1860 Upper Water Street, Halifax, NS 423-4405
$$ Major cards, wheelchair accessible, non-smoking area,
lunch Mon. - Fri., dinner daily
Owner Jim O'Carroll has had a loyal following in Halifax
ever since he arrived from Scotland. With offerings such as
Brotchan Buidhe, a favourite Gaelic-Irish soup, the menu
reflects his Celtic roots. Evening diners are treated to
traditional Scottish, Irish, and Cape Breton music.

Pastamimi 15
Spring Garden Place, Halifax, NS 423-2202
Quinpool Road, Halifax, NS 422-4448
$ Limited seating, mall hours (including Sunday afternoons)
These small outlets provide deli-style Italian selections to eat
on the premises or to take out. Their daily offerings of fresh
pastas, salads, quiches, etc. are inexpensive and delicious.
The Spring Garden Road location is on the lower mall level,
conveniently next to a fine wines outlet.

★ **Perks** 16

*1781 Lower Water Street, Halifax, NS **429-9386***
$ Open 24 hours daily, wheelchair accessible, non-smoking area

A good lunch stop or mid-morning break location offering speciality coffees, pastries and sandwich fare — quick and tasty. This is as good as the doughnut shop gets. Perks is conveniently located next to the ferry terminal in the heart of downtown Halifax.

Rocco's 17

*300 Prince Albert Road, Dartmouth, NS **461-0211***
$$ Major cards, not wheelchair accessible, non-smoking area, Mon. thru Friday lunch and dinner, Sat. and Sun. dinner only

Dartmouth is called the "City of Lakes" and this restaurant offers an unsurpassed view of the aquatic activities on Lake Banook. A native of southern Italy, owner/chef Rocco Scarola prepares to order many specialities such as Linguine al Pesto or Cannellone al Forno.

Ryan Duffy's 18

*5640 Spring Garden Road, Halifax, NS **421-1116***
$$-$$$ Major cards, call ahead for wheelchair assistance, non-smoking areas

Although they offer a varied menu, if you want the best steak in Halifax go to Ryan Duffy's. You choose the cut and size tableside and the chefs will prepare it to your request. Depending upon your mood you can be served in four areas — an intimate dining room, a more casual bar and grill, a club room, or a speakeasy.

Salty's on the Waterfront 19

*Historic Properties, Halifax, NS **423-6818***
$$ Major cards, limited accessibility, non-smoking area, open daily for lunch and dinner

Salty's, with its casual ground floor dockside bar and grill and more formal upstairs dining room, features specialities from the sea plus innovative pasta and meat entrées. Ask for a window table to ensure a harbour view unsurpassed in the city.

★ **Scanway Restaurant** 20

*1569 Dresden Row, Halifax, NS **422-3733***
$$-$$$ Major cards, not wheelchair accessible, non-smoking area, Mon. - Sat. for lunch and dinner

Unni Simensen offers patrons authentic Scandinavian fare from her homeland in this pleasant second-story restaurant conveniently located in the Spring Garden Road area. A consistently fine luncheon menu features homemade soups, and the best open-faced sandwiches in the city including many that feature fresh and carefully prepared seafood. Try the sliced moist chicken breast, curried mayonnaise, apricots, and fresh asparagus on a bed of salad vegetables and light rye. End your meal with one of Unni's delectable desserts. Scanway is enjoyable at all times, and is particularly suited for leisurely lunches.

★ The Silver Spoon   21
*1813 Granville Street, Halifax, NS **422-1519***
$$$ Major cards, wheelchair accessible, open for lunch and dinner, Mon. - Sat., non-smoking area
This restaurant is located in a handsome, newly renovated house amid the hotel and banking district in downtown Halifax. The ground floor café specializes in lighter meals and desserts, while the more formal upstairs dining room offers a varied, imaginative and often changing menu. At its best, nothing in Halifax can match the Silver Spoon for fine dinner dining.

Soup'er Sandwich   22
*1820 Hollis Street, Halifax, NS **425-3474***
$

You may have to battle the lunchtime office crowd but the food here is downright cheap and the quantities are huge! As the name implies, sandwiches, made to order, and home-made soups are the speciality.

Sweet Basil Bistro   23
*1866 Upper Water Street, Halifax, NS **425-2133***
$$ Major cards, not wheelchair accessible, totally non-smoking, 10:00 am to 10:00 pm daily
Unni Simensen offers a variety of dishes at her second restaurant, Sweet Basil, located on the Halifax waterfront. House specialities include a variety of salads, open-faced sandwiches, and pasta dishes. For more substantial fare choose from the dinner entrées which may include Cajun specialities or seafood treats such as Atlantic lobster Maritime style, but be sure to save space for the home-made ice cream, cheesecakes, or Unni's famous Florentines.

Tea and Temptations   24
*44 Ochterloney Street, Dartmouth, NS **464-9005***
$ not wheelchair accessible, daily 10:00 am - 5:00 pm,
Located in a small historic house on Dartmouth's Heritage Walk, this English-style tea room serves lunch and a variety of specialty teas. Warm scones, sweet breads, and desserts plus a small gift shop make it an ideal spot to rest during a busy day.

Upper Deck   25
*Privateers' Warehouse, Halifax, NS **422-1289***
$$$ Major cards, non-smoking area, not suitable for wheelchairs, open 7 days a week for dinner only
Once a privateers' warehouse, this restaurant with its stone walls and cosy alcoves is steeped in an atmosphere of the past. The dining here is first class, offering a varied menu with seafood presentation the house speciality.

ACCOMMODATIONS

For a complete listing of accommodations in the Halifax area, including bed and breakfasts, consult the *Nova Scotia Travel Guide* (see Useful Addresses and Information). Hostellers should contact Hostelling International Nova Scotia, Box 3010 South, 5516 Spring Garden Road, Halifax, NS, B3J 3G6; 425-5450.

Many establishments are members of Nova Scotia's Check In Reservation and Information Service (see Useful Addresses and Information). Membership is indicated by a check mark in the *Nova Scotia Travel Guide*. In general, the accommodations listed below are the best of their kind. All are open year-round, and most have distinguishing features that will enhance your stay.

Approximate prices are indicated, based on the average cost, at time of publication, for two persons staying in a double room (excluding taxes): $ = under $70; $$ = $70-$100; $$$ = more than $100.

Cambridge Suites Hotel 26, 1583 Brunswick St., Halifax, B3J 3P5; 1-800-565-1263 or 420-0555. Adjoining Citadel Hill in central Halifax, located between the Spring Garden Road area and downtown. Small suites with fridge and microwave, guest laundry, exercise room. Complimentary continental breakfast. $$$

Chateau Halifax 27 (a Canadian Pacific Hotel), 1990 Barrington St., Halifax, B3J 1P2; 1-800-441-1414 or 425-6700. Top-floor restaurant with sweeping view of the city and harbour. All amenities. Adjoins Scotia Square shopping mall. $$$

Delta Barrington 28, 1875 Barrington St., Halifax, B3J 3L6; 1-800-268-1133 from Canada, 1-800-877-1133 from USA or 429-7410. Close to Historic Properties and most attractions. Adjoins Barrington Place Mall, restaurants and pubs. $$-$$$

Halliburton House Inn 5, 5184 Morris St., Halifax, B3J 1B3; 420-0658. Small, elegant hotel. Registered Heritage Property incorporating three 19th-century townhouses in the South End, several blocks away from the Spring Garden Road area. $$$

Holiday Inn Dartmouth 29, 99 Wyse Road, Dartmouth, B3A 1L9; 1-800-HOLIDAY or 463-1100. Located at the Dartmouth end of the Macdonald Bridge. Many rooms have great harbour views. $$$

Inn-on-the-Lake, Box 29, Waverley, B0N 2S0; 1-800-463-6465 from Atlantic Canada or 861-3480. Two hectares (5 acres) of parkland with private freshwater beach and outdoor pool, courtesy shuttle to airport (10 minutes away). $$-$$$

Park Place Ramada Renaissance, 240 Brownlow Ave., Dartmouth, B3B 1X6; 1-800-854-7854 from Canada or 468-8888. Located on the highway leading to Halifax and close to the Burnside Industrial Park, this hotel is suitable for car-oriented visitors. $$$

Prince George Hotel 30, 1725 Market St., Halifax, B3J 3N9; 1-800-565-1567 or 425-1986. Central downtown location with all the amenities. $$$

Sheraton Hotel 31, 1919 Upper Water St., Halifax, B3J 3J5; 1-800-325-3535 or 421-1700. Luxury accommodation on the Halifax waterfront (ask for a room on the harbour side). Indoor pool, sauna, whirlpool. Casino as of 1995. Adjacent to Historic Properties, this is the best-located hotel for visitors interested in the downtown and harbour. $$$

GETTING THERE

BY LAND

The Trans Canada Highway enters Nova Scotia from New Brunswick. Visitors from the United States must pass through Canada Customs checkpoints before entering the country.

Greyhound from New York (1-800-231-2222) and Voyageur from Montreal (613-238-5900) connect with SMT bus lines in New Brunswick (506-458-6000). SMT connects with Acadian Lines (902-454-9321) which offers bus service to Halifax and other Nova Scotia destinations from Amherst.

VIA Rail Canada (1-800-561-3949) provides train service to Halifax via Montreal.

BY SEA

There are several options for car-ferry trips to Nova Scotia.

Portland, Maine, to Yarmouth, Nova Scotia

Daily service by *MS Scotia Prince* from early May through October. Reservations required. In Canada: Box 609, Yarmouth, NS, B5A 4B6. In the USA: Prince of Fundy Cruises Limited, Box 4216, Station A, Portland, Maine, 04101. In USA and Canada call toll-free 1-800-341-7540; in Maine, 1-800-482-0955. Yarmouth is about a 3-hour drive to Halifax.

Bar Harbor, Maine, to Yarmouth, Nova Scotia

Daily service from mid-June to mid-September aboard the *MV Bluenose*. Tri-weekly service during the off-season. In Canada: Marine Atlantic Reservations, Box 250, North Sydney, NS, B2A 3M3; 902-794-5700. In the USA: Terminal Supervisor, Marine Atlantic, Bar Harbor, Maine, 04609; 1-800-341-7981.

Saint John, New Brunswick, to Digby, Nova Scotia

Daily service across the Bay of Fundy aboard the *MV Princess of Acadia*; three trips daily during peak season. Marine Atlantic Reservations, Box 250, North Sydney, NS, B2A 3M3; 902-794-5700. In the USA, 1-800-341-7981. Digby is about a 2 1/2-hour drive to Halifax.

Prince Edward Island to Nova Scotia

Daily service between May 1 and December 20 from Wood Islands, PEI, to Caribou, NS. Northumberland Ferries, Box 634, Charlottetown, PEI, C1A 7L3; 1-800-565-0201 in NS or PEI. Elsewhere, 902-566-3838. No reservations. Caribou is about a 2-hour drive to Halifax.

Marine Atlantic operates a year-round daily ferry service between Cape Tormentine, New Brunswick (near the NS border), and Borden, Prince Edward Island. No reservations. Cape Tormentine, NB, is about a 3-hour drive to Halifax.

Newfoundland to North Sydney, Nova Scotia

Twice-daily, six-hour passage from Port-Aux-Basques to North Sydney (four times daily during peak). Bi-weekly 13-hour passage from Argentia to North Sydney, mid-June through mid-September only. Marine Atlantic Reservations, Box 250, North Sydney, NS, B2A 3M3; 902-794-5700. In the USA, 1-800-341-7981. North Sydney is about a 5-hour drive to Halifax.

BY AIR

Both Air Canada (1-800-563-5151) and Canadian Airlines International (1-800-665-1177) provide daily flights to Halifax from most Canadian cities. Affiliated regional carriers Air Nova and Air Atlantic offer scheduled connections within Atlantic Canada and flights to select destinations in the eastern United States.

Air Canada in partnership with Continental Airlines services destinations in the United States and worldwide through Houston, Newark, and Boston.

Car rentals may be arranged at the Halifax International Airport, and limousine service is available from the terminal buildings. The Halifax airport is located about 40 kilometres (25 mi.) northeast of the city, and the 30-40 minute cab ride costs about $30. An airport bus service to downtown hotels costs $18 round-trip, $11 one-way.

ATTRACTIONS

Following is a selective listing of many of the city's points of interest. Not all of these attractions are located along the designated walking tours.

Anna Leonowens Gallery, Granville St., Halifax; 422-7381 (Nova Scotia College of Art and Design).

Art Gallery of Nova Scotia, 1741 Hollis St. at Cheapside, Halifax; 424-7542.

Bedford Institute of Oceanography, located near Dartmouth side of MacKay Bridge, Halifax; 426-4093.

Black Cultural Centre for Nova Scotia, Route 7 at Cherrybrook Rd., near Dartmouth; 434-6223.

Bluenose II, often at Privateers' Wharf, Historic Properties, Halifax.

Brewery Market, Hollis and Lower Water Sts., Halifax; 429-6843.

Cathedral Church of All Saints, 1320 Tower Rd., Halifax; 423-6002.

Dartmouth Heritage Museum, 100 Wyse Rd., Dartmouth; 464-2300.

Fort McNab National Historic Site, McNab's Island; information, 426-5080.

Government House, 1451 Barrington St., Halifax. Lieutenant-governor's residence since early 1800s.

Grand Parade, between Barrington and Argyle Sts., Halifax.

Halifax City Regional Library, 5381 Spring Garden Rd., Halifax; 421-6983.

Halifax Citadel National Historic Site, overlooking downtown Halifax (you can't miss it). Group reservations, 426-5080.

Halifax Public Gardens, Spring Garden Rd., at South Park St., Halifax.

Historic Quaker Whalers' House, 57-59 Ochterloney St., Dartmouth; 464-2300 (Dartmouth Museum).

Historic Properties, on the Halifax waterfront.

Maritime Museum of the Atlantic, 1675 Lower Water St., Halifax; 424-7490.

Maritime Command Museum, Admiralty House, CFB Halifax; 427-8250.

Micmac Heritage Gallery, Barrington Place Shops, Halifax; 422-9509.

Nova Scotia Centre for Craft and Design, 1683 Barrington St., Halifax; 424-4062.

Nova Scotia Museum of Natural History, 1747 Summer St., Halifax; 424-7353.

Old Town Clock, at the base of the Citadel. Halifax's most famous landmark.

Old Burying Ground and Welsford-Parker Monument, Barrington St. (across from Government House), Halifax.

Prince of Wales Martello Tower, Point Pleasant Park, Halifax.

Province House, Hollis St., Halifax; 424-4661.

Shearwater Aviation Museum, at CFB Shearwater; 460-1083.

Shubenacadie Canal Interpretive Centre, 140 Alderney Dr., Dartmouth; 462-1826.

St. George's Church ("Little Dutch Church"), Brunswick St. at Cornwallis, Halifax; 423-4927.

St. George's Round Church, Brunswick St. at Cornwallis, Halifax; 423-4927 (damaged by fire June 1994; restoration underway).

St. Paul's Anglican Church, at the Grand Parade, Halifax; 429-2240 (office).

Uniacke House, Mount Uniacke; 866-2560.

York Redoubt National Historic Site, off Purcells Cove Rd., Halifax.

FESTIVALS

What follows is a listing of some of the best and most popular festivals and events in the city and surrounding area. Note that the scheduling of many of these events is subject to change; the Check In Reservation and Information Service will provide updated information (Tel. 1-800-565-0000).

May — **Moosehead Grand Prix** (Shearwater). International auto race.

May-June — **Scotia Festival of Music**. Internationally renowned festival of chamber music.

June — **Greek Festival**. Three-day feast put on by the Halifax Greek community.

June — **Multicultural Festival**. Food, music, and more. A ten-year-old celebration of the Metro area's multicultural community.

July — **Nova Scotia International Tattoo**. A musical extravaganza with a military flavour.

July — **Halifax Highland Games**. A Scottish festival with pipes and drums, heavy events, and more.

July — **Maritime Old Time Fiddling Contest and Jamboree** (Dartmouth). Top-notch competitors from Canada and the United States.

July — **Atlantic Jazz Festival**. Outdoor concerts and late-night sessions in city bars.

July — **Africville Reunion**. The spirit of the Black community of Africville is revived at a picnic, church service, and dance.

Aug. — **Buskers International**. Street performers including jugglers and clowns provide 10 days of fun along the waterfront.

Aug. — **Nova Scotia Designer Crafts Council Summer Festival**. A juried market draws many of the province's best craftspeople.

Sept. — **Shearwater International Airshow**. Atlantic Canada's largest demonstration of aerial acrobatics.

Sept.-Oct. — **Studio Rally Weekend**. Craft studios across the province open to the public.

Oct. — **Helen Creighton Folklore Festival** (Dartmouth). Celebration of folk music and art honouring Canada's best-known folklorist.

NIGHT LIFE

THEATRE

Halifax is home to Neptune Theatre, now in its fourth decade of performing live professional theatre, and Symphony Nova Scotia. Unfortunately, neither offers regular performances during the summer months. However, a surprising number of communities throughout the province, including Halifax, are summertime venues for live theatre. Many productions are distinctly Nova Scotian — revealing much about the province and its people.

Grafton Street Dinner Theatre, 1741 Grafton St., Halifax; 425-1961.

Historic Feast Company, Historic Properties, Halifax; 420-1840.

Jest In Time Theatre, 1541 Barrington St., Halifax; 423-4647.

Neptune Theatre, 5216 Sackville St., Halifax; 429-7070.

Rebecca Cohn Auditorium, Dalhousie University, Halifax; 494-2646. A variety of live performances including the Symphony Nova Scotia concert series and Neptune Theatre main stage productions for the 95-96 season.

Theatre Arts Guild, 6 Parkhill Rd., Halifax; 477-2663.

Wormwood's Cinema, 2015 Gottingen St., Halifax; 422-3700. Alternative film.

PUBS AND TAVERNS

Halifax's compact downtown area is crowded with drinking establishments, several featuring live Celtic music. For a less boisterous evening, enjoy a quiet drink at a restaurant or hotel bar. The legal drinking age is 19.

A K's Emporium, Brewery Market, 1496 Lower Water St.; 492-2441. Open Monday-Saturday 11:30am-8:30pm, Thursday-Saturday 11:30am-around midnight.

Harbourfront Bar, Sheraton Hotel, 1919 Upper Water St.; 421-1700. Open daily 11:30am-2am (closes early on slow nights).

Lower Deck, Historic Properties; 425-1501. Open Monday-Saturday, 11am-1am.

Midtown Tavern, 1684 Grafton St.; 422-5213. Open Monday-Thursday, 11am-11pm, Friday and Saturday, 10am-11pm.

Salty's, Historic Properties; 423-6818. Open daily 11:30am-11pm (slightly later on busy nights).

Split Crow Beverage Room, 1855 Granville St.; 422-4366. Open Monday-Wednesday 11am-12:30am, Thursday-Saturday 11am-1am, Sunday noon-10pm.

PARKS AND OUTDOOR ACTIVITIES

Point Pleasant Park, in the South End of Halifax. Shaded walking paths and views of Halifax Harbour and the Northwest Arm.

Hemlock Ravine Park, Kent Avenue, off the Bedford Highway (Route 2). Formerly part of the Duke of Kent's estate. Ideal for an afternoon stroll.

Sir Sandford Fleming Park (The Dingle), off Purcells Cove Rd., overlooking the Northwest Arm. Beautiful view of the Arm along walking trails. Dedicated in 1912, the Dingle Tower was built to commemorate 150 years of representative government for Nova Scotia.

Shubie Park, off the Waverley Road (Route 318), in Dartmouth. Nature trails and freshwater swimming highlight this municipally owned park and campground.

GOLF

Grandview Golf & Country Club (18-hole), Dartmouth; 435-3278.

Granite Springs Golf Club (18-hole), Prospect Road (near Halifax); 852-3419.

Oakfield Country Club (18-hole), Grand Lake (near Halifax International Airport); 861-2658.

DEEP-SEA FISHING

Options for saltwater fishing range from relaxing outings, often in combination with some cultural or historical commentary, where sedentary groundfish are the catch, to serious searches for large gamefish — bluefin tuna, shark, and bluefish. Murphy's Wharf (see Seasonal Boat Tours) is one of several charter companies that operate out of Halifax Harbour. For complete listings consult the *Nova Scotia Travel Guide* (see Useful Addresses and Information).

New Dawn Charters, 553 Purcells Cove Rd., Halifax, NS, B3P 2G2; 479-2900. A 12-metre (40-ft.) Cape Islander available for five-hour fishing charters. Catch cod and haddock off Chebucto Head and Sambro. Shark fishing by request.

SEASONAL BOAT TOURS

Murphy's on the Water, Cable Wharf, 1751 Lower Water St., Halifax; 420-1015. Harbour tours, some with commentary, aboard a variety of vessels.

USEFUL ADDRESSES AND INFORMATION

The *Nova Scotia Travel Guide* ("The Doers and Dreamers Complete Guide") is an indispensable aid to visitors. To obtain a copy write to Nova Scotia Tourism and Culture, Box 130, Halifax, NS, B3J 2R5 or call toll-free 1-800-565-0000. The Guide is also available at Visitor Information Centres throughout Nova Scotia.

It is possible to make detailed plans for your Halifax vacation before leaving home by contacting Nova Scotia's Check In Reservation and Information Service. Travel Counsellors will provide invaluable advice, reservation services, and a wealth of written material to make travel planning easier. In North America, call 1-800-565-0000 or write to Nova Scotia Information and Reservations, Box 130, Halifax, NS, B3J 2M7.